W9-DHM-694

MORE PARENTS ARE TEACHERS, TOO

ENCOURAGING YOUR 6– TO 12–YEAR–OLD

CLAUDIA JONES

WILLIAMSON PUBLISHING CO. CHARLOTTE, VERMONT 05445

**Library of Congress
Cataloging-in-Publication Data**

Jones, Claudia
    More Parents are teaches too :
encouraging your 6- to 12-year-old/
Claudia Jones
        p.   cm.
    Sequel to: Parents are teachers,
too. ©1988.
        ISBN 0-913589-43-8
        1. Child rearing.   2. Education,
Elementary—Parent participation.
I. Jones, Claudia. Parents are
teachers, too. II. Title.
HQ769.J7518   1990   649'.1—dc20

Cover design: Trezzo-Braren Studio
Interior design: Kehoe & Kehoe
    Design Associates
Cover photograph: David Nelson
Photography: David Nelson, Jack
    Williamson
Typography: LaserImage
Printing: Capital City Press

Williamson Publishing Co.
Charlotte, Vermont 05445

Manufactured in the United States of
    America

10 9 8 7 6 5 4 3 2

With special appreciation to Martha,
Kate and Allison Wool, and Zachary,
Sarah and Ryan Williamson.

Contents

Preface   **7**

Chapter 1 A Healthy Self-Concept   **9**
Middle Childhood: 6 to 10 Years
Preadolescence: 11 to 13 Years
Decision-Making
The Aggressive Child
A Sense of Family
Fostering Creativity

Chapter 2 Parent, Child, School   **39**
School Readiness
Learning Styles Differ
Identifying Your Child's Learning Style
Learning Problems
Special Education: The Pros and Cons
Homework

Chapter 3 The Joy of Reading   **71**
How To Sell Your Child on Books
Methods Used in Teaching Reading
Working With the Beginning Reader
Reading Problems
Working With the More Advanced Reader

Chapter 4 Language: Learning to Communicate   **99**
The Beginning Writer
Improving a Child's Writing Skills
Writing a Report
Computers
Spelling
Playing With Words
Writing Quotations
Parts of Speech
Creative Language Activities

Chapter 5   Math Can Be Fun!   **131**
Learning Math
When A Child is Having Trouble
Math Facts
Understanding Place Value
Math Processes
Math Strategies
Graphs
Estimating

Chapter 6   Creative Problem-Solving   **167**
Guess and Check
Looking for Patterns
Making a Systematic List
Making or Using a Drawing or Model
Eliminating Possibilities

Chapter 7   Fun With Science   **183**
Improving Science in Your Child's School
Encouraging Science at Home
Astronomy
The Amazing Human Body
Caring for Our Environment
Science Experiments and Activities

Chapter 8   Geography   **211**
Activities to Make Geography Fun
Creative Geography

Appendix   **218**

Bibliography   **220**

Acknowledgements

There are a number of people who have contributed a great deal to various sections of this book. My sincere thanks to

Sheila Lennon, for her enthusiasm, guidance, and invaluable input on the subject of reading,

Jane Mergy, for her thoughtful insights and helpful feedback on the topic of learning styles, and

Karen Hughes, for providing a sounding board for some of the sections on behavior and learning problems.

Thanks also to Roger Fox and Regina Carroll for sharing their materials on learning styles.

I would also like to thank my family — my parents, whose confidence in me has always been an important part of my successes; and my husband and son who have endured without complaint a long year of sharing me with a computer.

Finally, I want to thank Susan Williamson, my editor. Her skills in editing and her own avid interest in education resulted in comments and questions which forced me to dig deeper and produce a book which is far more complete and useful than it would otherwise have been.

To parents everywhere. May the joys and laughter of parenting far exceed the worries and frustrations.

Claudia Jones is also the author of *Parents Are Teachers Too: Enriching Your Child's First Six Years.* (Williamson Publishing, Charlotte, VT).

Rights & Permissions
Williamson Publishing Company and Claudia Jones gratefully acknowledge the granting of permission to quote, reference, and/or reprint from the following publications: *Any Child Can Write: How to Improve Your Child's Writing Skills from Preschool through High School,* McGraw-Hill, 1978; *Do You Know Your Parents?* by Dan Carlinsky, 1982, Price Stern Sloan, Inc., Los Angeles, California; "Don't Be Afraid To Fail," Copyright © United Technologies Corporation, 1986. *The 4MAT System: Teaching To Learning Styles With Right/Left Mode Techniques,* by Bernice McCarthy, copyright 1980, 1987 by Excel, Inc. (Excel, Inc., 200 West Station Street, Barrington, Illinois 60010.). "*Games for Math: Playful Ways to Help Your Child Learn Math, From Kindergarten to Third Grade,*" by Peggy Kaye, Pantheon Books, 1987. *How To Discipline With Love (From Crib to College),* by Dr. Fitzhugh Dodson, © 1977, 1978 by Dr. Fitzhugh Dodson. Reprinted by arrangement with New American Library, a division of Penguin Books U.S.A., Inc., New York, NY. *The Learning Child: Guidelines for Parents and Teachers,* by Dorothy H. Cohen, Copyright © 1972. Quoted with permission from Pantheon Books; "Learning How to Learn," by Pat McNees; "Make a Moon Calendar," by Susan Ballinger, *Science Scope,* February/March 1988. "Night Time is the Right Time," by Bob Riddle. Reproduced with permission from *Science and Children* (Nov/Dec 1988). Copyright 1988 by the National Science Teachers Association, 1742 Connecticut Avenue, NW, Washington, DC 20009; *100 Ways to Enhance Self-Concept in the Classroom,* by Jack Canfield and Harold Wells, Copyright 1976, pp. 53, 127, 129, 157. Adapted by permission of Prentice Hall, INc., Englewood Cliffs, New Jersey; "Presenting Forewards Backwards," by Drs. Rita and Kenneth Dunn. Reprinted with permssion of the publisher, Early Years, Inc., Norwalk, Connecticut 06820. From the October 1988 issue of *Teaching/K-8.* Problem Solving in Mathematics — Grades 5 & 6 (Lane County Math Project), Copyright 1983. Problems used with permission from Dale Seymour Publications, Palo Alto, California. (Problems are found on pages 168-182.); "A School Where Learning Styles Makes a Difference," by Patricia Lemmon, Copyright 1984, National Association of Elementary School Principals; Science Activity Book — A Smithsonian Family Learning Project, copyright © 1987, Galison Books. Activities on rock candy crystals and leaf pigments adapted with permission of GMG Publishing Corporation, 25 West 43rd Street, New York, New York 10036. "Singular Peanuts," by Edward Donovan, Science Scope, January, 1989. *Smart Kids With School Problems: Things to Know and Ways to Help,* by Patricia Vail, E.P. Dutton, 1987. *A Whack On the Side of the Head: How to Unlock Your Mind for Innovation,* by Roger von Oech, Copyright © 1983, Warner Books, Inc. "What Parents Should Do For Their Kinds," by Patrick Welsh, *U.S. News & World Report,* May 26, 1986. "Who Am I?" activity, by Dr. Sidney Simon; adapted with permission of the author. "Why We Need to Understand Science," Copyright© 1989, Carl Sagan. All rights reserved. First published in *Parade.* Reprinted by permisson of the author. *Your Child's Self-Esteem,* by Dorothy Corkille Briggs, Doubleday & Co., 1970.

Preface

As a child walks out the door on that first day of school, his parents often feel an acute sense of anxiety and sadness. He suddenly looks so small and innocent. Is he really ready? Are we ready, they wonder, to turn him over to a teacher whom we don't know for six or seven hours a day, five days a week? Yet, once the child is on his way, there is also a sense of relief.

Congratulations! You made it through the ups and downs of the preschool years! As a parent, I understand these conflicting emotions. As a teacher, I hope that from the first day of school onward you realize that your job is not done. When a child begins school, the parenting role simply enters a new phase.

Most parents accept their role as teachers while their children are preschoolers. Unfortunately, too many assume that once their child enters elementary and middle school, they can "retire" from the teaching profession.

With each school year, children are presented with increasing amounts of information. This means an increase in the number of chances for misunderstanding or missing a concept and falling behind. Children become frustrated when a problem is not perceived early and dealt with quickly. Self-esteem plummets and poor behavior results. An alert parent can prevent a child's disillusionment with school and with himself.

Understandably, many parents find their lives very structured and overscheduled. They often feel guilty about the lack of time spent with their children. This book offers ways to make the time parents have with their children count. Fifteen minutes of individual attention can do amazing things for a child.

The school-aged child is growing ever more thoughtful, asking meaningful questions, making perceptive observations, and considering varied points of view. Once a child can read and write, the number of available learning games increases tremendously. The opportunities for parent and child to interact positively and have fun together are endless. Parents can teach their child by including him in everyday activities requiring the use of not only academic skills, but motor skills, creative thinking, and deductive reasoning skills as well. In this way, learning becomes part of life, not just an exercise done in school.

More Parents Are Teachers, Too describes the various stages of development that parents can expect their children to pass through during middle childhood and preadolescence. It provides suggestions for enhancing a child's self-concept and explains the value of identifying a child's preferred learning style.

More Parents Are Teachers, Too emphasizes the importance of parents actively working to ensure that their children receive the best and most effective education possible. Most important, the book includes lots of activities and games that incorporate learning and skill-building into home-life. More than anything, that is the goal of this book — to help parents and children have fun learning together, to embrace learning as part of life, not separate from it.

Claudia Jones

Note: For reasons of simplicity, I refer to both the parent and the child in the masculine throughout the book. No sexism is intended. I simply find writing "he or she" or making the parent or child male in one chapter and female in the next, distracting. Teachers, on the other hand, are referred to in the feminine, which in elementary school is still the case more often than not.

CHAPTER ONE

A Healthy
Self-Concept

A Healthy Self-Concept

Children who feel good about themselves learn more easily and are more successful academically than children with poor self-concepts. Conversely, children who perform well academically tend to feel good about themselves. The close link between self-esteem and performance is indisputable.

A child's self-esteem influences and is in turn influenced by a great many other things — how lovable and special he feels, his relationship with parents, siblings and peers, how comfortable he is making decisions, and his capability to meet the expectations of others and to set and attain his own goals.

It is extremely important for parents to put a considerable amount of effort into helping their children develop positive self-concepts. *A positive self-concept is perhaps the most important prerequisite for success as a student and human being.*

Because each child is unique, the parent's role in strengthening self-concept varies from child to child. However, there are ideas to consider, words to say, and activities to try which increase the probability of a child being happy and well-adjusted.

Understanding the stages of a child's intellectual, emotional and social development helps parents provide appropriate experiences and create realistic expectations. While children don't develop at the same rates, they do progress through similar stages of growth at some time in their development.

Don't concern yourself with whether or not your child is doing at a certain age what he is "supposed" to do. Much more helpful for you, the teachers and the child is being able to recognize that perhaps your child has not gone through a particular developmental stage yet and is not quite ready for the next. Struggling with algebra? Maybe he has not yet progressed through Piaget's period of formal operation. Having trouble with phonics? Maybe he is not yet ready to decode symbols. Knowing and understanding developmental stages can save you and your child a lot of undue stress. It's almost always appropriate to say, "Let's wait a few months until my child is ready to learn this new concept."

Middle Childhood: 6 to 10 Years

Middle childhood is considered a period of emotional equilibrium, especially when compared to the previous ups and downs of the preschool years and the more turbulent stages of preadolescence and adolescence yet to come.

Although family remains important to the child, it no longer plays the central role in his life. In addition to his role in the family, a child now finds himself assigned two new roles — student and member of a peer group. Identity is tied to all three roles, and self-esteem depends not only upon accomplishments at home, but also upon achievement in school and peer acceptance.

Your child may decide during this time that you are suddenly incapable of knowing the answers to anything. It is not uncommon for him to transfer the role of "omniscient one" to his teacher. He may find it great fun to catch you making an error. Although he may decide to choose the parent of the same sex as a model, don't feel crushed if he chooses his role models and heroes from the world of athletes, television and movie stars, musicians or older adolescents he knows. He is becoming aware of adulthood waiting in the future. He wants to understand the ways of the grown-up.

Entering middle childhood means added pressures. At school there are new expectations, both intellectual and behavioral. Students are expected to follow directions, sit still for instruction, and accept their teacher as the authority figure. They are treated more often as members of a group and less often as individuals. Additionally, they are asked to master academic skills and are evaluated on their merits relative to other children.

The Role of the Peer Group

Peer groups play an increasingly important role in the development of a sense of self. Dorothy Cohen (*The Learning Child*) explains: "In coping with the need to sustain and strengthen their sense of themselves as individuals, children now turn to other children as natural allies in a common cause. They band together to establish themselves as the coming generation, separate from that of their parents." Evidence of the importance of peer groups is seen in the clubs which children form, complete with their own hierarchies, rules, rituals, and secrets.

Peer group acceptance is a vital part of a child's social development. From his peers a child learns how to relate to others, and his sense of adequacy depends on his ability to master such skills as cooperation, competition, and the art of compromise. Consequently, a child who lacks these basic skills may be rejected or cruelly tormented. Even the most socially adept child will experience some difficult trials while seeking acceptance by contemporaries. Eventually, however, most children find a place among their peers.

An important job of the 6- to 10-year-old is learning the rules of the peer group, as he is constantly judged by how well he adheres to those rules. According to Dorothy Corkille Briggs, author of *Your Child's Self-Esteem*, "Playmates force a child to face the realities of his world. In short order and in no uncertain terms, they teach what is acceptable and what is not. 'You brag too much' 'I don't want to play with a cheater!' 'Quit griping; he didn't mean to do it!' 'Drop dead!'" As tactless and cruel as it can be, the peer group nonetheless provides a child with a much-needed structure as he begins to separate himself from his parents and develop his own identity.

Intellectual Growth

Middle childhood marks a noticeable increase in children's mental capabilities. During their preschool years, a period labeled by Swiss psychologist Jean Piaget as the *preoperational period*, children deal with the world on a very concrete level. They need to physically manipulate objects in order to gain an understanding of different concepts. Somewhere around the age of 6 or 7, children become capable of dealing with symbols, manipulating things mentally rather than just physically. This added mental ability characterizes what Piaget calls the period of *concrete operations*. During this period, children's reasoning capabilities expand, and they learn to operate according to rules (academic as well as social). This growth opens up a whole new world of challenges and experiences, making formal education possible.

For example, decoding words (phonics), with its symbols (letters) and rules, involves a more advanced intellectual ability than the sight-reading activity which usually occurs at an earlier stage. The basic skills of math are also based on rules which dictate, among other things, place value and the sequential steps to be taken in adding, subtracting, multiplying, or dividing.

During middle childhood, children gain the ability to make deductions about relationships. (If Alan is older than Meg, and Meg is older than Jason, then Alan is older than Jason.) This is an important step in logical thinking. Children are also able to, and most love to, classify anything and everything. Encouraging all sorts of collections will help a child learn to make more and more subtle distinctions between things and people.

Another milestone in the 6- to 10-year-old's intellectual development is the new-found ability to grasp the concept of *reversibility*. He will be able to understand that a ball of clay which has been elongated into a snake can be reshaped into a ball, and that subtraction reverses addition.

As children become more logical, their thinking becomes less magical. They develop a more realistic sense of time, and a strong interest in the functioning of the human body. They exhibit a general thirst for knowledge, characteristic of middle childhood. This endless curiosity in the world and how things work makes it easy to interest the 6- to 10-year-old in learning activities.

Despite the acquisition of more advanced mental abilities, your child still makes mistakes in reasoning which show that the transition to logical thinking is not yet complete. Although his involvement with school and peers continues to grow, remember that *family is still an important part of his life.* Dr. Barbara Biber describes this child as "looking for ways to belong to his family and feel free of them at the same time." This is not unlike the experience of a teenager. For all his yearnings for independence, this child is still a child, not a miniature adult. The acceptance by and love of his parents and family remain crucial to his sense of self.

Preadolescence: 11 to 13 Years

As your child enters preadolescence, sometime around the age of 11, you are likely to find yourself dealing with a child you hardly recognize. First comes a time of discord and discomfort, when your child tests the limits of your authority and seems to have a perpetual chip on his shoulder. Dr. Fitzhugh Dodson describes this period as one where the child "suddenly becomes obnoxious in every way you can think of...This stage usually hits parents with a wallop. Your stable, reasonable, well-behaved child seems suddenly to have taken an overdose of Obnoxious Pills. Your most reasonable parental requests...will be met with surly outbursts of irritation or snotty remarks."

Somewhere around the age of 12, things tend to become a bit easier, at least temporarily. The 12-year-old is generally more positive, outgoing and enthusiastic than he was at 11. He is more tolerant of others and sympathetic, and able to relate successfully with both his parents and his peers. At the same time, he begins to assert that he is no longer a child, and may become more intellectually and athletically competitive with his parents.

As your child turns 13, or thereabout, he changes again. Most noticeable is a turning inward, a preoccupation with self. Hershel Thornburg describes this age as "the least happy of the emerging adolescent years." The 13-year-old is moody, extremely self-conscious, and private. He withdraws into his room a lot, in need of privacy as he worries about his present self and his future. A parent's attempts at discussion may be viewed as prying. This is a difficult time for a child, as he begins to question his relationship with his parents from whom he has learned and on whom he has depended so much.

Physically, the preadolescent is undergoing dramatic changes in height, body configuration and facial proportions. This stage of pubescence indicates that his body is nearing puberty and sexual maturation. He experiences great anxiety and concern as he compares his own body to that of his peers. At a time when he wants more than anything to conform, the preadolscent must deal with his lack of control over the rate or end results of his physical growth. Access to accurate information about these physical changes is important.

Intellectual and Social Growth

The ability to think abstractly increases in preadolescence. This is the beginning of Piaget's period of *formal operations*, when children start to reason things out, to hypothesize about situations and perceive cause and effect relationships. They are not dependent on concrete objects to help understand basic ideas, and they can deal with symbols on a higher level than was possible in middle childhood. The ability to classify objects becomes more sophisticated. They can now group animal species based upon similarities of anatomy, and classify body parts according to function. Not only can preadolescents use grammar correctly, they can think about it. Earlier they learned to attach words (symbols) to objects, now they can group these symbols according to function. (Words such as "boat," "house" and "tree" can now be grouped together under the classification of "nouns.") They can apply what they already know about culture to current problems in society as well as deal with the more complex mathematical concepts of fractions, basic algebra, and geometry.

Socially, preadolescents remain very much under the influence of their peer groups. They become more aware of the individual personalities of their peers. An interest in the opposite sex begins to emerge, especially among girls. Most peer relationships and real friendships are still with members of the same sex, however, and cliques, especially among girls, are common. Preadolescents are aware of and annoyed by the capriciousness of group membership and show a desire for "real friends." Friendship is of the utmost importance.

There has been a trend in education to focus attention on these middle years between childhood and adolescence. The result has been the development of the middle school concept, where preadolescents are given the intellectual challenges they need, in an appropriate environment, without the social pressures to enter adolescence before they are ready. Middle school programs take into account the physical, emotional and social, as well as the intellectual development of children. As schools re-examine curriculum and physical plants, middle school programs need to be considered. The appendix lists publications which explain the purpose and goals of middle schools, and provide a more thorough understanding of preadolescents.

Responding to the Preadolescent

Needless to say, these years of preadolescence, especially the eleventh and thirteenth, are difficult for the parent as well as the child. But each stage plays an important role in the child's development. This period is more easily accepted if parents understand that children need to express some wild behavior while growing more independent. Parents must also accept the inevitability of losing control over their children. As frightening as these changes are, they are all part of the process of child development, repeated from generation to generation.

Experts in child psychology advise parents of preadolescents to not panic. Try to avoid lecturing, and instead, listen, reserve judgment, and accept youthful thoughts for what they are. It is extremely important that parents make a real effort to maintain open communication with their children. For instance, when your child expresses his desire to adopt an unusual hairstyle, your first reaction may be to forbid it. Stop, instead, and ask yourself where this action stands in the scheme of things. Is controlling your child's self-expression worth the risk of alienation? I think, generally speaking, you'll find it's not. *If the ability to talk with a child is lost during preadolescence, the chance of regaining it later is slim.*

Be honest with your child if you're not sure about something. He will probably tell you, if you ask, whether or not he is comfortable with a particular situation. If you sense any anxiety on his part about his ability to deal with a situation, take control yourself. *Don't ask him to grow up before he's ready to.*

Parents who create opportunities to pursue enjoyable activities with their preadolescents increase the chance of maintaining an emotional rapport. Going to movies, sporting events, or on camping trips together reminds your child that you are still there for him.

Some Things We All Need

Although your elementary school child may seem more interested in the world of his peers, he still needs to know that to you he is special, a worthwhile and lovable human being. Hugs, smiles, and the words, "I love you," said sometimes with tenderness and sometimes with boisterous affection, all send a message your child needs to hear.

In addition to providing affection, a parent needs to express confidence in his child's ability to succeed. The child who hears his parents describe his accomplishments with pride feels good about himself. He approaches new activities with an "I can do it" attitude. Listen to yourself when you talk to your child. Do you praise him or his work? Focus your comments, positive and negative, on the deed and not the child. "Wow, does the yard look nice! You did a great job mowing!" is better than "What a good kid you are for mowing the lawn!" Children need to feel they are "good" no matter what.

Children are sensitive to what is said and how it is said. Therefore, be honest in your praise, and don't go overboard or express feelings you don't genuinely have. Try to make your comments specific. Whenever possible, relate a successful experience to a specific strength. (When you tell your child, "These answers are all correct! You remembered to borrow each time," you not only confirm his achievement, you also reaffirm your confidence in his ability to learn a new process.)

A child also needs to feel that his teacher, as well as his parents, believes in him and likes him. If you sense otherwise, talk with both your child and teacher. Find out why your child feels the way he does, and enlist the teacher's help in remedying the situation.

Encourage your child to describe the successes he experienced during the day, and share them, perhaps at the dinner table or at bedtime. You may have to help at first. Point out the things he accomplished (cleaned his room, got a hit in a baseball game, finished his homework, read a story to his younger sister, learned how to tie a square knot, etc.), and help him see that he does indeed learn and succeed every day.

One of the most important ways a parent tells his child he is special is by choosing to spend time really talking with him. Below are some activities which encourage discussions between parent and child. They have been developed for the purpose of enhancing self-concept by exploring attitudes and behavior, as well as considering alternatives.

In order for these activities to succeed, you need to create an atmosphere of mutual trust, where your child feels safe in sharing his feelings. Most important, you must really listen. Your child needs to know that you will accept his contributions and thoughts without judgment.

Self-Esteem Activities

➤ Choose a quiet place to play a sentence completion game. Take time to share the thoughts and feelings behind the answers. If you will take the time to draw your child out, you may find that just one sentence will lead to a lengthy and revealing discussion. For example:

Parent: If I start a sentence, will you finish it?
Child: O.K.
Parent: I am happiest when...
Child: I am happiest when I'm playing.
Parent: Playing what?
Child: Baseball, with my friends.
Parent: Which friends do you most like to play baseball with?
Child: Charley, Brett, and Peter.
Parent: Are they your best friends?
Child: Yes, but sometimes Peter acts kind of bossy. He always wants to be the pitcher.
Parent: What do you do when he gets bossy?
Child: We tell him to quit it.
Parent: And he does?
Child: Yes, because he knows if he doesn't, we won't play with him.

Parent: What is it that you like so much about playing baseball?

Child: I just like playing!

Parent: Yes, but what specifically is the best part?

Child: I guess just running around a lot and yelling and hitting homeruns.

Parent: I think I know what you mean. Sometimes when I'm walking across a big field, I just want to stretch my legs out and run as fast as I can!

This conversation could easily continue for a while longer. By the time it ends, the parent discovers a little more about what makes his child tick — who his friends are, how he deals with them, the fact that he prefers group activities to individual ones, and so on. The child learns that his feelings are important and that his parent understands them. Here are some other discussion starters:

★ If I could have one wish, it would be...

★ I get angry when...

★ One question I have about life is...

★ People think I am...

★ I think I am...

★ I don't like people who...

★ I appreciate...

★ Something I do well is...

★ Something I am getting better at is...

★ I don't like people to help me with...

★ People who expect a lot from me make me feel...

➤ A family activity to build self-esteem: Each person folds a piece of paper in half length-wise and writes his name on the top line of each half. Each person first lists his own good qualities and the things he likes about himself on the left side. Then he passes his paper to the person on his right, who writes down, on the right side of the paper, what he sees as the person's strengths. Continue passing until the papers are returned to their "owners." Each person should compare the lists and ask, "Do people see me the way I see myself? How can I encourage others to see more of my strengths?"

In a group whose members are comfortable expressing feelings and exploring ideas, an individual might ask, "What is it that I do that makes you think I'm courageous?" That might, in turn, lead to an interesting revelation to all involved — that often what we observe or perceive is not necessarily what another person is feeling or trying to communicate.

> Help your child make a personal time line. Draw a vertical line down a piece of lined paper, writing the child's birth on the top line. Help him recall and record significant events in his life (include events such as learning to walk, starting school, childhood diseases, travel, new brothers and sisters, losing pets, and so on). Many of life's major milestones are passed over as something everyone does. A timeline helps a child see just how much he has learned and accomplished. Once he feels good about what he has done, he is apt to be more willing to look for new areas to explore.

January 5, 1980	I was born!
10 months old	started walking
August 10, 1982	My sister Julie was born.
March 1984	I got the chicken pox.
Summer 1985	My first bicycle
September 1985	I started Kindergarten - Mrs. Green, teacher
November 1985	I was ringbearer at Uncle Mark's wedding.
Summer 1986	Camping at Yosemite; a trip to Disneyland
September 1986	First Grade - Mrs. Stowers, teacher
February 1987	I broke my leg skiing.
September 1987	Second Grade - Mrs. Amren, teacher
Christmas 1987	A new puppy - Henry!

➤ **Who Am I?:** Ask your child to fill out an autobiographical questionnaire. Consider including some or all of the following:

★ Name

★ Date of birth

★ List 10 words that best describe you (he may want to ask others in the family for their input on that)

★ How do you spend your free time?

★ Who are your best friends?

★ Who is your favorite older person?

★ What do you see yourself doing in 10 years? 20 years?

★ What are your favorite T.V. shows? movies? songs?

★ What is your favorite book?

★ What are your hobbies?

★ What do you think of school? your teacher?

★ Are you happy with the person you are? If not, what would you like to change?

For an added dimension, suggest that your child take some photos to record in pictures who he is at this point in time. Not only would it be interesting to talk with your child about his answers, but it would also be fun to save the questionnaire and photos and repeat the activity periodically to note any changes. To make the activity even more effective, consider answering the same questions yourself, and share your answers with your child.

➤ Suggest that your child make a collage about himself. Look for pictures and words to cut out of magazines. Once completed, ask him to explain his choices of pictures and words.

➤ Encourage your child to draw a self-portrait. Get paper and pencils and sit together in front of a mirror for this activity.

➤ Ask your child to complete the following:
    If I were a(n) animal (tree, T.V. show, flower, musical instrument, insect, color), I'd be a _____, because _____.

Example:
    If I were a boat, I'd be a Sunfish, because I like the quiet solitude of sailing.

➤ Take a "Trust Walk" with your child where one of you is blindfolded, and the other is the guide. The walk is to be completed in silence, with the guide's job being to look out for his partner's safety, while making the walk as interesting as possible. After returning to the starting point, change places. Share your reactions to each role. Which was easier? What was it like being blindfolded?

➤ Discussion starters:

★ Ask, "What is the nicest thing you ever did for someone else? that someone else did for you? that you did for yourself?"

★ Does your child know how he was named? Explain what his name means to you. How does he feel about his name? Does it "fit"?

★ What does your child think is "The Perfect Age"? Why?

★ What does your child consider the most beautiful part of his body? the ugliest part? What does the expression "You can't judge a book by its cover" mean to him?

★ Ask your child who he admires greatly. Can he explain why?

★ If a long-lost, wealthy relative died and left your child $500,000, what would he do with it?

★ Ask your child to fill in the blanks in as many different ways as possible: I used to be ___, but now I'm ___.

★ Ask your child how he feels about the world around him, the environment, what would he like to do to change the world, what can he do now?

★ Look for *The Kids' Book of Questions*, by Gregory Stock, Ph.D. It is full of short, thought-provoking, sometimes silly questions which are meant to get children thinking and talking.

★ An important component of a child's self-concept results from his perception of how he influences others. If you set a good example for him, he will learn to relate to others in a thoughtful and considerate manner. Ask your child what kinds of things he feels he might do to make others feel good about themselves?

★ Discuss "pull ups" and "put downs," words which can either make another person feel good about himself ("I sure appreciate your help." "You'll get it next time!") or feel inferior and incapable ("I can't believe you struck out!" "Boy, are you dumb!").

★ Read with your child, books like *The Original Warm Fuzzy Tale*, by Claude Steiner, and *I Am Lovable and Capable*, by Dr. Sidney Simon.

Expectations and Goals

Developing realistic expectations is a difficult but important parental task. A child reads a lot into his parents' expectations for him. If expectations are too low, the child thinks his parents feel he is incapable of accomplishing more. If expectations are too high, the child is frustrated by repeated failures and filled with feelings of worthlessness.

When setting expectations, the parent must look at the total child as objectively as possible, considering strengths and weaknesses, interests, and present emotional situation.

When in doubt, lean toward higher expectations with this understanding: Children want to live up to their parents' expectations. They enjoy a reasonable challenge. Beware of placing unreasonable pressures on your child, and be sure he understands that your expectations and his performance are not connected with your love for him. Children are confused about this, and fear that poor school or athletic performance equals loss of love.

With an older child, sit and discuss your expectations. Be sure to listen to his thoughts, and talk about any misgivings he might have. If he feels uncomfortable with your expectations, explore these feelings. Try to determine if your expectations are indeed too high, or if your child is trying to avoid failure by choosing a "safer" goal. If it seems reasonable, change the goal, lower or raise the expectation. Be flexible! Or, perhaps you can compromise — set goals just slightly higher than what your child feels comfortable with, and encourage him to "stretch" a little further. This way, he will experience success, but still know there is more to be accomplished. You want your child to experience the satisfaction that comes with real accomplishment.

Help your child learn to set goals for himself. Goals which are too large, too long range and too difficult to achieve are bound to result in negative feelings. By helping a child choose challenging but attainable goals, you provide valuable opportunities for him to see himself as a "doer," capable of success.

Instilling Values

A child isn't born with values; parents teach them — right vs. wrong, honesty, integrity, trust, thoughtfulness. In school, teachers usually reinforce the same basic values. Conflict arises when the values and behaviors learned from parents and teachers don't conform to those subscribed to by peers. As the child grows toward adolescence, the conflicts and inconsistencies increase.

Parents need to be models of the values they want to instill. The clearer you are about your own values, the easier it is for your child to recognize, understand, and adopt them. Children want clear direction from parents.

Pose some "what if?" situations to your child and ask him to offer his thoughts. For example, "What if you saw your best friend steal a pack of gum from the store?" If his reactions turn out different from yours, ask him to explain his reasoning, and listen without criticism. Then present your own views and reasoning. Leave your child with something to think about. As long as you keep the lines of communication open, your child will discuss the issues with you at another time. The less you try to force your opinion on him, the more likely it is that he will eventually come to agree with you.

Decision-Making

In today's society, with its increase in stress-related illnesses, teenage suicides, teenage crime, drug use and pressure to experiment sexually, children need to be able to make smart decisions and to know when to say, "No." Like anything else, making good decisions takes practice. The more decisions a child makes, the more aware he becomes of their consequences, and the more skillful he becomes at decision-making in the future. This means you need to let your child make "bad" choices. That's how he learns! For example, allow him to decide whether to spend or save his money, what afterschool activities to participate in, what television shows he most wants to watch, whether he wants to do homework right after school or play for an hour first. *Children need to feel a certain amount of control over their own lives.*

A more difficult kind of decision-making comes to play in situations involving peer pressure. Parents spend a lot of time and energy trying to teach their children the difference between right and wrong, a definite set of values. What good are those values if a child does not have the self-confidence and the ability to maintain them under pressure? You can ease your mind a little by teaching your child to be assertive, to respond the way he really feels is right for him. Without this kind of assertiveness, a child is likely to join in activities and do things he really doesn't feel good about. As a result, he loses self-esteem. Spend some time talking with your child about the following three types of behavior.

Non-assertive behavior is when a person allows others to violate his rights or violates them himself. Such behavior usually allows the person to momentarily avoid an unpleasant situation. Non-assertive behaviors often result in lowered self-esteem, and feelings of resentment. A person who buys something he doesn't really want because the salesperson spends alot of time with him is exhibiting non-assertive behavior. Loaning someone a bike or money, drinking alcohol, or skipping school when you don't really want to but just can't say "no" are also non-assertive behaviors.

Assertive behavior involves the expression of one's rights, honest opinions, feelings and needs in such a way as to not infringe on the rights, opinions, feelings and needs of others. An assertive person does not make others do as he wants; he feels satisfied that he has made known who he is and what he needs. Verbal and non-verbal assertive messages are generally accompanied by eye contact, a calm manner, and an appropriate tone of voice. Assertiveness includes saying "No" and making it stick.

   An example would be when a person refuses the offer of a cigarette, saying, "No, thanks. I don't want to smoke," repeating the words, if necessary, in a calm but self-assured manner until the other person stops offering.

Aggressive behavior involves expressing one's rights, needs, opinions and feelings combatively, with no regard for the feelings of others. Aggressive behavior is often indirect, expressed through sarcasm, gossip, secrets, manipulation and spitefulness.

As human beings, we all have the following rights. Aggressive behavior should not infringe upon these rights. The right:

★ to make and refuse requests

★ to express opinions

★ to not have to justify one's feelings

★ to be treated fairly

★ to make mistakes and accept the consequences

★ to express annoyances and anger in non-aggressive ways

★ to give compliments and express affection

Talk about these rights with your child. Discuss situations you anticipate he will eventually have to deal with. Does he ever feel pressure from his friends? from adults? How has he responded in the past to these pressures? What are the alternatives in the future? Ask your child, "What kind of friend would push you to do something you didn't want to do?" (The kind you don't need!)

While you discuss with your child his right to be an assertive person, remind him of the need for self-control, to see that he doesn't go too far and end up being aggressive. He must remember everyone else's right to be assertive also. He needs to learn consideration and thoughtfulness for those around him. Without concern for others, we become aggressive and manipulative.

Choice Activities

➤ **Consider the choices:** Help your child see that there is always more than one possible choice in any situation. While in the car or finishing dinner, try as a family to come up with alternatives for the situations below. Brainstorm to discover things you could do, not necessarily what you would do.

★ You get to school and notice you have a hole in your pants.

★ You're at someone's house for dinner and you don't like the main dish.

★ Someone stole something from you and you think you know who it is.

★ You hear that your friend has told a lie about you.

Role-playing: Role-playing provides valuable practice in learning to deal with pressures from others, to say "no" and make it stick. It is one of the best ways for children to practice being assertive. (Examples: How would you deal with someone trying to talk you into smoking marijuana? drinking a beer? stealing a candy bar? going someplace your parents have said is "off limits"? staying out past your curfew? making fun of someone with a handicap? teasing an animal? cheating on a test?)

Start by taking the part of the aggressive peer who is trying to pressure your child into doing something he doesn't want to do. Try switching roles later, so that he can see how effective an assertive response can be.

While role-playing, encourage your child to:

★ Ask questions: "What are we going to do there?"

★ Name the trouble: "That's illegal. That's against my family rules." Emphasize that it is O.K. for your child to "blame" you for his behavior. "My parents won't let me."

★ Identify the consequences: "We could get hurt. We could be arrested. I'd be grounded."

★ Suggest an alternative: "Let's go over to my house and watch TV." At the same time, he should physically start walking toward his house and try to sell the idea. "We'll make popcorn and ask Bill over."

★ Leave, leaving the door open: If his friend still won't give up his plan, your child can say, "If you change your mind, I'll be at home."

The Aggressive Child

Some parents find themselves dealing with a different problem — their child is aggressive. The aggressiveness may be physical (fighting, pushing, threatening) or it may be verbal (bossy, manipulative, sarcastic). Aggressive behaviors are expressions of feelings of inadequacy. Lectures and punishment only serve to convince the aggressive child that he is a disappointment to his parents. His defenses only grow stronger. A child's behavior is directly related to his feelings about himself. Until the child develops a healthy self-concept, his behavior and progress in all areas are likely to reflect his feelings of self-doubt.

Parents of an aggressive child need to look as objectively as possible at their child. They need to consider what the child experiences daily at home and at school. He may not be receiving as much positive feedback as he needs. Difficulty with schoolwork, poor athletic skills, and a need for more attention all contribute to a child's lack of self-esteem. Aggressive children need to experience some success in life. They need to feel their parents are proud of what they do well. They need help in overcoming difficulties in school and mastering basic skills. They need their parents' unconditional love.

Many aggressive children don't understand the difference between what is acceptably assertive, and what is unacceptably aggressive. Aggressive children can role-play various situations in order to practice new behaviors. Parents can begin talking about situations which cause trouble. What is the child's perception of the problem? How would he respond to a certain problem? Then, switch roles so the child can see how the parent handles the same situation, using assertive rather than aggressive behavior.

In helping a child deal with his aggressiveness, encourage him to pay attention to how others involved in a situation are feeling. An aggressive child tends to focus on himself and his own feelings; he needs to learn to cue in to the feelings of others as well.

As he works on learning to speak to and deal with children and adults more appropriately, a child might like to set up a chart on which to keep track of instances in which he uses assertive tactics instead of aggressive ones. (This is a basic behavior modification technique and can be effective if parents stick with it.) In other words, each time his parent (or teacher) notices him being assertive in a situation where he would normally have been aggressive, the child gets a star (or sticker or whatever) on his chart. The chart makes his progress concrete. There should be a reward of some kind given once the child has earned a certain number of stars. At least once a day, the parent should talk with his child about each instance for which he earned a star. It's important that the child hear that his parent is proud of him. He needs to know that his parent recognizes the effort he is making to change his behavior. Only when the child becomes truly aware of his behavior, and sees the benefits of changing it (that positive attention is more satisfying than negative), will he be able to control it.

If discussion, role-playing, charts and praise don't bring results, a parent may want to check into getting some counseling for his child. The ultimate goal should be to find the cause of the aggressive behavior and help the child develop the sense of self-confidence that he needs in order to behave acceptably.

A Sense of Family

Certainly today, the nuclear family that many of us grew up in, is no longer the norm. But whether one is married, a single parent or a stepparent, the goal should remain the same — to provide one's child with a sense of belonging, of being a contributing and valued member of the family.

There are a number of things parents can do to create a strong sense of family. For instance, whenever plausible, children should be involved in decision-making which will affect the entire family (choosing a pet, planning a vacation, and so on). Children should be assigned appropriate household chores. Although they may gripe and moan about jobs to be done, children with chores feel good about being responsible, contributing members of their families. Hectic schedules often make it difficult for families to participate in activities together. As a result, parents must make a real effort to unite its members. Below are some suggestions to consider.

Family Activities

➤ Consider a surprise day off for the whole family, where everyone "plays hooky" and does something special together.

➤ Some evening after dinner, get the family photo albums out and share memories. Discuss the different feelings that are evoked by photos. Talk about what it means to be a family. Share pictures of you when you were young.

➤ Using a large piece of posterboard and felt-tipped pens, work together to develop a family timeline to show the important events in the family's history. Leave room to add future events. Encourage everyone to contribute to the project. Post the timeline where it can be seen. (In a stepfamily, the first part of the timeline might have two separate lines which then meet to make a single line at the point where the two families became one.)

➤ Make plans for a special "family night" and make popcorn and/or a special dessert.

Tell your children that they get to ask you questions, but the "trick" is that first they must guess what your answer will be. This is a good time for siblings to talk things over, offer opinions and share in "solving a problem." When the children are through with their questions for you, you will get a chance to ask them some questions. You, too, must first guess what answer you think each child will give.

Keep two rules in mind: 1) a person may choose not to answer a question, and 2) play only as long as people are having fun.

Questions for Children to Ask Their Parents
(from Dan Carlinsky's *Do You Know Your Parents?*)

★ Would you prefer to play: tennis, bridge, golf, or Monopoly?

★ Do you usually: brush your hair, comb your hair, or brush and comb your hair?

★ Did you have a nickname as a child? Your nickname was _____.

★ What is your favorite meal? breakfast, lunch, or dinner.

★ How many states have you visited? less than five, between six and ten, or more than ten.

★ In how many cities have you lived? just one, two or three, or four or more.

★ How many of the Seven Dwarfs can you name? none, two or three, four or more.

★ Can you juggle three oranges or other objects?

★ If one parent was offered a great new job opportunity in another state, would the other parent move reluctantly, move willingly, or insist on staying where they live now?

★ Did you go to your high school prom? yes or no.

★ If you needed emergency surgery and the surgeon turned out to be a woman, would you feel: uneasy, perfectly neutral, or relieved?

★ What is your favorite comic strip?

★ Did you have any pets as a child?

★ (Without looking) What color are your spouse's eyes?

★ Can you name at least one of your spouse's friends from childhood?

★ If you won half a million dollars in a lottery or sweepstakes, would you: quit your job, take a vacation and then go back to work, or keep right on working?

★ If you could live anywhere in the world, where would you pick?

★ Within 5 pounds, how much do you weigh?

Questions for Parents to Ask Their Children:

★ What is your favorite subject in school: math, reading, other?

★ Can you stand on your head: yes or no?

★ If you could watch only one television show a week, what would it be?

★ What is your favorite color?

★ Who is your best friend?

★ Which frightens you most: spiders, the dark, or dogs?

★ Give or take two inches, how tall are you?

★ If you suddenly inherited a thousand dollars, what would you want to do with it?

★ Do you know how your name was chosen?

★ What was the most enjoyable thing you have done in the past year?

★ What would be your ideal dinner?

★ What is your favorite movie?

★ If you had to be one or the other, which would you rather be: uncomfortably hot or uncomfortably cold?

➤ Individual letters to grandparents, aunts, uncles or cousins provide connections to a whole other set of people who can offer a new sense of belonging in the world beyond one's own neighborhood.

➤ Videotape special family events or everyday activities to send to distant relatives and friends. Creative videotaping, which can provide several days of inventive fun, allows children to get into set design, scripting, costumes, and plot evolution. These home dramas are great fun, terrific learning experiences, and delightful surprises for relatives who get to view them.

Fostering Creativity

By encouraging a child to think creatively, parents provide opportunities for him to grow in self-confidence. He learns that he can control the outcome of various situations if he is willing to take chances, investigate, experiment.

In his book entitled *A Whack On the Side of the Head*, author Roger von Oech says, "I believe that the mind is not only a computer that processes information, it's also a museum that stores experiences... a playground in which to play, a muscle to be strengthened, a workshop in which to construct thoughts." Too often we, as a society, pressure children and adults alike to follow the rules, stop playing and get down to business. Unfortunately, this attitude stifles innovative thinking. We need to make an effort to teach our children to take creative risks, to play with ideas, and always consider, "What else could this be?"

A parent who wants to foster creativity in his child should:

Encourage curiosity and imagination. Any time a child discovers an unusual or different use for an object, let him know you heartily approve. "That's smart thinking! What a good idea!" You want to encourage being able to see beyond the obvious.

Allow time to daydream. Offer a penny for his thoughts when he is looking particularly pensive. Talk to him about the ideas he has and pictures he draws. Ask questions to show your interest.

Ask a lot of "what if" questions. ("What if the earth rotated around the moon?" "What if people didn't need to eat?")

Show how errors can be stepping stones to new ideas. An error tells us it's time to change tactics, look in another direction. ("If you're not failing every now and then," says von Oech, "it's a sign you're not being very innovative.")

Eliminate any pressure to conform. Focus instead on the joy of creating, be it an idea, a picture, a story or an invention. ("I bet you had fun doing this. Did you?")

Encourage careful observation. Although he may not have immediate use for the knowledge he gains, he may in the future. Any time he has a problem to solve, the more ideas he has to draw upon, the better.

Respond to creative efforts with care. It's important not to judge and thereby risk squelching the flow of ideas.

Daring to Put Creativity to Use

Our world has an abundance of problems to be solved. If solutions are to be found, it is vital that we nurture independent and creative thinking in our children. We can start by encouraging them to become interested and involved in seeking to better their community, their environment. This might mean organizing an anti-litter campaign in your neighborhood and cleaning up the roadsides or a nearby park. It could mean writing a petition to get library hours changed or a stop sign put up on a dangerous street corner.

We need to do what we can to encourage our children to take an interest in current events, to learn what they can about different issues, and then to take action. Talk with your child about how or why problems arise and discuss alternative solutions. Watch for examples in the news of people who are working for a cause.

Too many of us are content to be followers. We need more leaders, more individuals who think for themselves, people willing to take risks, look for answers and strive to make improvements. How we perform as individuals will determine how we perform as a nation.

Books Can Help

Each year in a child's life presents new conflicts, more decisions and an awareness of increasingly complex emotions. Trying to discover where he fits into the world around him is not an easy task.

Books can be a tremendous help to children, as they are to adults. Books help children recognize emotions and choices, and offer ideas on how to handle both. They can watch the characters in a book to see how they react and deal with their conflicts and worries. When you read to your child and talk about the books, you offer a safe and impersonal way to discuss any subject which is of concern to him.

The following books might help your child deal with particular situations in his life. There are certainly many more to be found in the library or bookstore. Children also receive reassurance and help from stories which have no main focus, but which present a picture of childhood to which he can relate.

Each title has a letter (P for primary grades, I for intermediate grades, and A for Advanced readers) to identify the reading level of the book. It will help you in searching for books for your child to read on his own. When reading to your child, his age and individual needs are important rather than reading ability. Skim through a book first to see if it is appropriate for your child before you begin reading.

Divorce

It's Not the End of the World, Blume (I-A)
My Dad Lives in a Downtown Hotel, Mann (I)
The Boys and Girls Book About Divorce, Gardner (for 9- to 12-year-olds)

Sibling Relationships

Me and Caleb, Meyer (I)
Me and Caleb Again, Meyer (I)
Tales of a Fourth Grade Nothing, Blume (I)

Peer Relationships

The Meat in the Sandwich, Bach (I)
Me and Fat Glenda, Perl (I)
The Ears of Louis, Green (I)
Ellen Tebbits, Cleary (I)
Iggie's House, Blume (I)
Otherwise Known as Sheila the Great, Blume (I)
Last Was Lloyd, Smith (I)

Death

Annie and the Old One, Miles (P-I)
A Summer to Die, Lowry (A)
A Taste of Blackberries, Smith (I)
Bridge to Terabithia, Paterson (A)
Nana Upstairs & Nana Downstairs, de Paola (P)
The Tenth Good Thing About Barney, Viorst (P)
There Are Two Kinds of Terrible, Mann (I-A)
Saying Goodbye to Grandma, Sewall (I)
Blackberries in the Dark, Jukes (I-A)
Mama's Going to Buy You a Mockingbird, Little (A)
I Had a Friend Named Peter, Cohen (P-I)
The Accident, Carrick (P-I)
How It Feels When a Parent Dies, Krementz (A)

Handicaps

David in Silence, Robinson (A)
Me Too, Cleaver (I-A)
Mine For Keeps, Little (I-A)
My Brother Steven Is Retarded, Sobol (I)
What If They Knew?, Hermes (A)

Growing Up/Adolescence

Are You There, God? It's Me, Margaret, Blume (A)
Then Again, Maybe I Won't, Blume (A)

Parent, Child, School

T W O

Parent, Child, School

On the wall above my desk is a print of a Norman Rockwell painting given to me by my mother. In the picture, a teacher stands in front of her classroom, coat over her arm, gazing at her students. On the floor is an eraser and a smear of crushed chalk. The backs of the children's heads are pure Rockwell — a little girl with braids, boys with cowlicks and skinny necks. It's clear that the students are watching anxiously for their teacher's reaction to the messages they have written on the board. "Happy Birthday Miss Jones! Surprise! Surprise! Happy Birthday Jonesy!"

I don't think the students have been disappointed. On Miss Jones' face is a smile of genuine affection. I would be surprised if there weren't also a rather large lump in her throat. It is the kind of moment that makes teaching one of the most wonderful professions there is. And clearly, Jonesy knows it.

I think we all wish for our children a teacher like Rockwell's Miss Jones, who loves her students and wouldn't trade her job for anything. She is the kind of teacher whose enthusiasm and caring make learning fun. For her students, going to school each day is a positive experience, something to look forward to.

In reality, however, not all teachers are Miss Joneses and chances are our children will not find themselves in ideal classroom settings each and every school year. But there are things parents can do — involving both immediate and long range goals — to help make their child's school experience better.

School Readiness

O ne of the first important questions many parents must consider is whether or not their child is ready to start school. First grade is rigorous. Teachers have a curriculum to follow and students need to perform adequately on the standardized achievement tests given at the end of the year. Not surprisingly, students and teachers feel pressured.

For many children, the first grade curriculum and the pace at which new skills are presented present no problem. But there are a significant number of 6-year-olds who are not ready for the rigors of first grade. They may be less mature than the rest of the class — cognitively, socially, emotionally, as well as physically (motor skills). These children, when they encounter a program for which they are not ready, experience failure and a rapid decrease in self-confidence and self-esteem. This is not the positive introduction to school that we envision for our children.

Chronological age is not always an accurate indicator of a child's readiness for school, but it gives us a place to start. Most states have raised the age requirements for entering first grade from 6 by November or December, to 6 by August or September. *Whenever your child's birthday falls, base your decision concerning when to send him to school on his readiness rather than his age.* Boys in particular are often not developmentally ready for school when they turn 6, and need an extra year before they are ready for formal instruction.

Some of the skills which a child should have before entering first grade include his ability to: state his complete address, listen to a short story and answer questions about it, repeat an eight to ten word sentence (said only once), identify what things are made of, count eight objects correctly, relate holidays to the correct seasons, cut with scissors, tie a shoe, and copy a triangle. A child who is unable to do most of these things is probably not yet ready for first grade. For a more complete checklist on readiness, talk with a kindergarten or first grade teacher, or send for *Ready or Not! The School Readiness Handbook* (see appendix for more information).

If you are concerned that your child may not be ready for first grade, after considering his age and his skill level, meet with his kindergarten teacher to discuss the situation. What options does the school offer? Is there a transition class (a "prefirst" for children who have completed kindergarten but aren't ready for first grade)? Or would your child need to simply repeat kindergarten? Some schools offer a pre-kindergarten class for children who are old enough but not ready developmentally for school.

It's difficult for some parents to avoid feeling guilty if their child is not ready for school; somehow they think they have failed. The real failure, however, would be not giving a child the extra time he needs. *The most important consideration in this matter must be what is best for the child.* A parent who finds himself having to make this decision should keep in mind the following:

★ Research shows that although some younger first graders do as well as their older peers, they would have fared better had they waited a year. Studies have also found a correlation between too early placement in school and diagnosed learning disabilities as well as generally poor social and emotional adjustment.

★ Most parents whose children spend a year in prefirst or repeating kindergarten are convinced by the end of May that the decision to give the child another year was the right one.

★ Chances are that a child who is not ready for first grade will feel a sense of relief at not being pushed into it.

An extra year gives a "not-quite-ready" child time to mature and a chance to develop a sense of confidence in his ability to learn and succeed. Then, when he begins first grade, the child is much more likely to find it a positive and enjoyable experience.

A Positive Attitude

To succeed in school, a child needs a good self-concept and a positive attitude toward school and education. He gets both from his parents before he ever begins school and each requires continuous supervision and nurturing throughout the school years.

When I was growing up, the value of education was never questioned in our home. Rather, we accepted school as a generally pleasant fact of life. Being students was a job which we were expected to do well, and, for the most part, we did. Our parents made themselves available to help if needed, were happy to quiz us for tests, and posted our successes on the kitchen bulletin board. They also gave us each leeway to accomplish work in our own way.

The fact that you are reading this book means that education is already important to you. Be sure you communicate this to your child. Be supportive of the school and get to know his teacher(s). If this year he doesn't have a teacher like Rockwell's Miss Jones — if he has one who is not exceptional, but adequate — help him learn to make the most of the year anyway. Don't let him dwell on the negative aspects of school; help him discover the positive instead. *Your own attitude can make all the difference in how your child deals with school.*

The Value of Mistakes

In her book, *Smart Kids With School Problems: Things To Know and Ways To Help*, Priscilla Vail writes, "Active learning depends upon willingness to take risks, acceptance of the error half of trial and error, and openness to ideas." A child who doesn't understand the value of mistakes thinks he can avoid failure by taking the easy way, yet, avoiding failure may also mean avoiding learning and growing.

Parents must make it clear that they don't expect 100 percent, A's, or perfection all the time. Children need to be assured that mistakes are O.K., that they are not only a normal part of learning, but that they can be very helpful!

Certainly we don't want a child to think it's all right to make mistakes repeatedly, but we do want him to be willing to take chances, try new things, knowing that an error increases the possibility of eventual success. The point we want to get across is that the value of mistakes comes in what we can learn from them.

The following was published in the *Wall Street Journal*, by United Technologies. Read it with your child and talk about the message.

Don't Be Afraid to Fail

You've failed many times, although you may not remember. You fell down the first time you tried to walk. You almost drowned the first time you tried to swim, didn't you? Did you hit the ball the first time you swung the bat? Heavy hitters, the ones who hit the most homeruns, also strike out a lot. R.H. Macy failed seven times before his store in New York caught on. English novelist John Creasy got 753 rejection slips before he published 564 books. Babe Ruth struck out 1,330 times, but he also hit 714 home runs. Don't worry about failure. Worry about the chances you miss When you don't even try.

© United Technologies Corporation, 1986

A difficult situation arises when a bright child proudly shows his parent a paper marked 83 percent. While the parent's initial reaction might be, "Why isn't it a 93 percent?", it helps to evaluate the situation before offering any such remark. The parent might say instead, "You look pleased with your grade. Was it a particularly difficult assignment?" In this way, the parent invites the child to describe the situation. It's possible that the child learned more from the experience than the grade seems to indicate. And ultimately, isn't learning the goal of education?

It may well be that 83 percent was one of the highest grades in the class. Or it may turn out that the assignment or test had posed a particularly great challenge for your child, in which case he deserves congratulations, and the grade should be considered secondary to the child's success in meeting the challenge.

If it appears that the child is expressing satisfaction with a grade which could and should have been higher, the parent and child need to talk. It may be time to re-evaluate goals together, as well as the child's methods of study and use of free time.

Learning Styles Differ

"There was a youngster named Pete who had given his teacher and parents problems with constant hyperactivity, failure to follow directions, and a resentful attitude. We learned...that Pete was a visual rather than an auditory learner. He could not listen for any length of time and, when he did listen, he could not remember much of what was said.

His teacher began writing his assignments and placing them on a corner of his desk. Suddenly Pete was doing his work. He was a lot happier— and so was his teacher! We shared our knowledge with Pete's parents, who quickly put it to good use. For several years Pete had exasperated his parents by his failure to follow directions. After listening to Pete's teacher describe her success with visual instructions, his mother decided to try a similar experiment at home.

The next day she left a note on the refrigerator telling Pete what he was expected to do when he came home from school. When she returned home, he had done everything on the list. Delighted, she asked, 'Pete, how come you did all that?'

'Because that's what you *told* me to do,' he replied."

The above is one example of the many positive results reported by educators who recognize the need to provide for individual differences in the way children learn. It is because of differences in genetic make-up and experience that each of us develops our own unique learning style. *A parent who makes the effort to identify both his own and his child's learning styles, and then uses this information, significantly increases his child's chances for success as a student and as a person.*

Research on Learning

In recent years a good deal of research has been conducted in the area of learning style. These studies reflect the findings concerning the functions of the right and left hemispheres of the brain. Briefly, the left hemisphere of the brain is generally considered to be functioning when a person is involved in activities such as handwriting, language, reading, phonics, listening, and following directions. Such activities require logical, analytic thought and the use of symbols. The right hemisphere of the brain, on the other hand, is functioning when a person is involved in math computation, spatial relationships, sports, music and singing, artistic expression, and creativity. People with a dominant right brain respond intuitively and randomly to things and need concrete materials to manipulate. Physical movement accompanying a mental activity often helps these individuals in learning new skills.

It has become increasingly clear that a child who is right brain dominant tends to have a certain amount of difficulty in school, where most learning involves left-brain activity.

Dr. Rita Dunn, Director of the Center For Study of Learning and Teaching Styles of St. John's University in New York, has conducted extensive research on learning styles. Dr. Dunn and others have found that in addition to how one's brain processes information, there are a number of other factors which contribute to one's learning style. These include the physical environment, the social aspects of learning, the child's needs for structure and guidance, time of day, mobility and snacking.

Dr. Dunn and her husband, Dr. Kenneth Dunn, describe four types of cues used by an individual to perceive and interpret information — visual (through sight), auditory (through hearing), tactile (through touch and manipulation, also referred to as tactual), and kinesthetic (through combining the absorption of information with physical movement). They also explain that a person tends to process information either analytically or globally. "Analytic students are concerned with details, rules, procedures and directions; they like specific, step-by-step instructions. Global students, on the other hand, are concerned with end results and need overviews and the big picture; they like general guidelines, variety, alternatives, and different approaches."

Bernice McCarthy, in *The 4Mat System: Teaching to Learning Styles With Right/Left Mode Techniques*, presents a slightly different approach to dealing with learning styles. McCarthy combines many of the findings of researchers in different fields to create four basic groups of learners: Imaginative, Analytic, Common Sense and Dynamic. She focuses on the need to teach to all four learning styles: "Although each learner has a 'home-base,' a preference for learning... by using all approaches, students will gain more confidence and strength in the other kinds of experiences; will develop an awareness of the advantages of each way of knowing."

A third approach to learning styles is presented in Thomas Armstrong's book, *In Their Own Way: Discovering and Encouraging Your Child's Personal Learning Style*. Following a model created by Harvard psychologist Howard Gardener, Armstrong describes seven kinds of intelligences: linguistic, logical-mathematical, spatial, musical, bodily-kinesthetic, intrapersonal and interpersonal. He believes that millions of children who have been labeled learning disabled during the past 25 years are not in fact disabled, but have not been taught in accordance with their own learning style.

Although the various approaches to learning style have distinct differences, they are similar in certain fundamental ways. Each recognizes and utilizes the findings of research conducted on the right and left hemispheres of the brain. Consequently, each discusses the existence of auditory, visual, tactile and kinesthetic learning. A further similarity is the role played by the social and motivational needs of the individual in the development of his own learning style.

According to McCarthy, Armstrong, the Dunns and many others, *achievement improves significantly when students are taught through their individual learning styles.* Children with behavior problems (like Pete, described earlier) often show dramatic and positive changes when their learning styles are identified and appropriate programs developed. Entire schools, elementary through high school, have instituted learning style programs into their curriculums with encouraging results. These findings are exciting and deserving of attention by parents and educators.

Identifying Your Child's Learning Style

A parent who makes the effort to discover the various characteristics of his child's learning style can help his child in several ways. First, he can explain things and present new concepts in ways that the child is most likely to understand. Second, he can help his child recognize how he learns best and how to deal with information presented through a different style. Third, the parent can talk with his child's teacher about his findings and ask her cooperation in maximizing the benefits of this information. And fourth, once a parent knows his child's strengths, he can help him work on his weaknesses. By the time a student reaches high school, the great majority of his classes will be lectures. If a child is not an auditory learner, he will need to learn how to compensate for this prevalent learning situation.

While numerous formal learning style inventories are available and utilized by counselors, psychologists and educators, I believe a parent can identify his child's learning style using the method suggested below.

★ Spend time observing the child in different situations, watching for "clues" described below, and keeping a record of your observations.

★ Do an informal assessment by asking the questions suggested below and recording the child's responses. (First complete the following assessment as you think your child will respond; then compare your answers with your child's.) Be sure to tell your child before you begin, what you're doing. Let him know that there are no right or wrong answers. You might practice by asking a few unrelated questions such as, "Which do you prefer, a baked potato or french fries?" or "Would you rather swim or go rollerskating on your birthday?"

As you ask your child the questions below, note which style of learning your child prefers. By the end of the section, a definite preference of one or two styles usually becomes clear.

Remember that no child is strictly a one-style learner. He processes information in all four ways. You simply want to determine the most comfortable method(s) of learning. Teaching through preferred styles will result in the greatest learning.

★ Would you rather watch a video of a story or act out the story yourself? (*visual or kinesthetic?*)

★ Do you learn better when you read to yourself or when someone else reads to you? (*visual or auditory?*)

★ Would you rather listen to a cassette tape about something or play a game about it? (*auditory or kinesthetic?*)

★ Would you rather draw a picture about a story or put on a skit about it? (*tactile or kinesthetic?*)

★ Would you rather write a story or build a diorama about it? (*visual or tactile?*)

★ Do you understand directions best when the teacher explains them to you or when she shows you what you're supposed to do? (*auditory or visual?*)

★ Would you most like to tell someone about a story or build a model showing part of it? (*auditory or tactile?*)

Additional Clues

Faith and Cecil Clark, directors of the Human Development Clinic, have found that eye movement can be a cue to learning style. When you ask a right-handed person what his first memory is, for example, and his eyes look up as he thinks about it, chances are he is primarily a visual learner. If his eyes look sideways, he may well be an auditory learner, and if his eyes look downward and sideways, he probably tends to be a kinesthetic learner.

★ A child with illegible handwriting is more apt to be an auditory than a visual learner.

★ A child who responds with "Huh?" a lot, is more apt to be a visual than an auditory learner.

★ A child who has a hard time copying from the chalkboard is more apt to be an auditory than a visual learner.

★ A child who would rather show than tell you how something works is likely to be a tactile learner.

★ A child who likes to make things with his hands is most likely a tactile learner.

★ A child who seems to need to move around while learning is most likely a kinesthetic learner.

★ A child who is great at mimicking the mannerisms and behaviors of others, who is gifted athletically (gross motor skills) or who is gifted at fine motor coordination (drawing, typing, fixing things, and so on) is apt to be a kinesthetic learner.

★ If you hand a child a new toy or an old broken appliance, how does he approach it? Does he turn it over, check out each part, find what's movable and what's not? (tactile) Or does he look at it carefully and wait for you to show him what it can do? (visual)

Physical Environment

For many children, room temperature or the amount of sound or light in the environment may not matter either way. However, the child who shows strong preference for certain environmental conditions should be accommodated if possible.

Noise Level: Is it easier for you to work when the house is very, very quiet, when other people are talking quietly, or when there is a lot of noise? Some children may actually work best listening to music with headsets on, while others benefit from earplugs or earmuffs to create silence.

Lighting: Watch first to determine in what kind of lighting your child usually chooses to work — bright light, or more subdued light — and then ask him if he is aware of preferring one over the other. Some children work more comfortably by the natural light provided by a window, while others like an intense light source nearby.

Temperature: If you could choose to work in a cool place or a warm place, which would you choose? Your child may prefer to sit by a window where he can feel a cool breeze when it's hot, or sit near a source of heat if the house is chilly. Help him become aware of whether he feels comfortable or uncomfortable in certain situations. Talk about how to make any setting more comfortable.

Setting: Where do you most like to work when you do your homework or read a book? Some children need and prefer to sit at a desk or table to work, while others like to lie on the floor, sit on the bed or curl up in a chair.

Time of Day: Adults often refer to themselves as "night owls" or "morning people," acknowledging the fact that some people work better in the morning and others late at night. The same is true for children. Knowing your child's preference is particularly useful in trying to schedule homework time. Studies suggest that flexible scheduling which allows children to take achievement tests during their "best time of day" results in noticeably higher scores.

Social Considerations: Does your child like to study in his room alone, or does he prefer being around others when he works? Some children like to do their homework in the kitchen or family room where they can get immediate feedback to ideas and have some level of activity around them. Observation and honest discussion can tell you how your child learns best. Most children are surprisingly clear about which social environment works best for them. What is important to remember is that *learning a concept while part of a group is no less valid than learning the concept independently.* What counts is that learning is taking place.

Motivation and Persistence: Some children are much more strongly motivated to complete a task than others. Their persistence to stay on task is rewarded by task completion and praise. These children feel good about completing assignments and like to show their work to their parents. A parent's attitude and interest have a lot to do with the child's motivation to do well at school. Continual encouragement is important.

Structure: Does your child prefer to organize his own study situation, resisting an adult dictating how he should do his work? Or does he feel more comfortable if an adult provides specific guidelines and directions to follow? Most children are able to tell you what they need to learn best. Sometimes children welcome help. They may say, "I wish I could sit still longer," or "There are so many other things to do." That's your cue to help devise systems for self-discipline so your child doesn't become frustrated.

Food: Research indicates that both the grades and attitudes of some children improve if they are permitted to nibble on food while learning. It may be that a child who chews on his fingernails or his pencil actually needs something to snack on. Offer a plate of healthy snack food (preferably vegetables such as carrot and celery sticks, cauliflower, cucumbers) for munching while studying. If the intake of food is helpful, the child will seek out the plate of snacks. If the novelty wears off after a few days, food is not an important factor in his learning. And if food becomes an excuse to daydream, then it's safe to assume that food is more of a distraction than anything else.

Use Your Findings to Help Your Child

Take time to discuss with your child your findings about his learning style. He needs to be a partner in his education. It is very important that the child understand that while he may learn differently from his friends, this doesn't mean that he learns any less well or the wrong way. Invite him to ask you for help whenever he has trouble with a new skill. Then show him how to approach the problem in another way, using his primary learning style. Below are some things to keep in mind.

★ A visual learner should be provided with lots of pictures, maps, diagrams, charts, and art activities. Encourage him to ask for illustrations and graphic explanations when he needs something clarified, and to include his own illustrations in the notes he takes. Help him to begin drawing math word problems, diagramming in science and grammar. You'll notice he will begin to "sketch" much of what he learns.

★ It helps a visual learner to read ahead in any subject area where he has trouble. In this way, he will be familiar with the material before he hears it in a lecture and more likely to be able to ask the questions which will help him the most. As he reads, he might like to highlight words in a favorite color, or take "notes" by drawing pictures, or creating mnemonic devices to help him remember a concept.

★ An auditory learner benefits from hearing the words he is reading. Encourage the auditory learner to read aloud softly to himself in order to hear and grasp the words he is reading.

★ It is most helpful for an auditory learner to hear a lecture first and then read material and take notes.

★ If your child is not an auditory learner, encourage him to learn to write quickly, so he will be able to take adequate notes to help compensate in the upper grades when most information will be presented orally. Help him practice taking notes by jotting down only the important details as he listens to the news or to you as you read a short article from a magazine or book.

★ A tactile learner needs to be given opportunities to do things with his hands — make things and take them apart, do puzzles, play board games, construct models. A parent and child together can make Bingo and Concentration games to help in almost any subject area. Math with manipulatives is very helpful, and even grammar and sentence structure can be taught tactilely by physically moving word cards around, or setting punctuation marks in place correctly.

★ A tactile learner seems to pay attention better when his hands are doing something. If your child is a "doodler," don't automatically discourage the activity. Doodling may be his way of helping himself concentrate.

★ A kinesthetic learner needs to participate in sports, drama, pantomime, demonstrations, and role-playing. He may learn more easily if he taps things out or walks back and forth while repeating facts or spelling words. Using rhythms or playing word games like "Categories" often helps kinesthetic learners.

★ Some children learn most easily if ideas or facts are sung or chanted. These children should be encouraged to create raps or songs that include information they are studying.

★ According to Dr. Rita Dunn, children who read poorly benefit from dim or natural lighting. It seems to encourage relaxation and concentration. A controversial study reports that learning disabled children read better with tinted lenses, as the lenses help eliminate excess light which causes word distortion.

★ A child who prefers to work alone does his best learning when allowed to figure things out at his own speed, in his own way. He may enjoy self-checking materials which allow him to learn from his mistakes and progress at his own speed. Often these children flourish with a personal computer which reinforces correct choices.

★ Take the time to identify your own learning style, and become aware of how you normally present information to your child. People usually teach from their own mode of learning, and find it difficult to cross over to another. Accept the challenge of making the necessary adjustments in order to help your child learn most easily.

★ It can be helpful to have an older child help a younger child who has a similar learning style; it gives a wonderful boost and sense of confidence to both!

★ Keep in mind that learning styles may change as a child matures and as he grows older he will be expected to work with information presented in a variety of manners. Consequently, you want to provide activities which require your child to use all styles of learning, as well as teach him how to take information presented one way and put it into a more effective format to meet his learning needs. From time to time, reassess your child's learning style so that he can see the ways he has progressed and learned to compensate.

Share Your Findings

Communication between home and school is an important part of a child's education. Parents must be their children's advocates. If your child is already experiencing difficulty in school, it is especially important that you make an effort to identify his learning style. Then make an appointment to meet with his teacher and discuss your findings. (It is important that your child attend the conference, as he is the one with the most at stake.) If, for instance, you determine that your child is a visual learner, ask his teacher if it is possible for her to provide directions in writing as well as orally. Chances are your child isn't the only one who would benefit. If, on the other hand, your child needs information explained orally, ask the teacher if she will read through or explain her directions as she hands out a sheet with written instructions. In both cases, ask her to demonstrate and illustrate as much as possible, what she expects. Let her know you realize it may mean extra work for her, but explain your reasoning.

Encourage the teacher to ask your child from time to time to explain a difficult concept using his learning style. This allows the child to demonstrate his particular skills and recognizes that different learning styles are equally valid.

If your child is a kinesthetic learner, you have probably heard time and again that he has a hard time staying in his seat. He would benefit from his teacher's use of the techniques described for kinesthetic learners. Not only will the child's attitude and work probably improve, but the teacher's job will also become easier and more successful. Sometimes the solution can be as simple as letting a child stand at a table instead of sitting at a desk. The room to shift weight or move his paper up and down a table can be a tremendous help to the kinesthetic learner.

We've all been told how much simpler a task becomes when we use the proper tools. *For many children, learning style becomes a question of providing the right tools for each child.* If a seemingly bright child is floundering, it may be because he hasn't been given the right tools, in which case learning style is an area that deserves immediate attention. It is very possible that using what you know about your child's learning style, you, your child and his teacher can together make a child's "problem" manageable.

If a problem seems to persist, however, or you feel it might be more serious, check into obtaining a professional assessment of the situation. This should include a complete physical — it seems that some learning problems are caused by serious allergies or hypoglycemia. If your child's problem doesn't respond to a change in teaching styles and isn't caused by a physical problem, it is important to obtain further professional help in order to deal with the problem as soon as possible.

Activities to Build Basic Skills

The following activities deal with skills which are basic to the learning process. Approach the activities as games and keep it fun!

Auditory Discrimination

Think of a category such as animals (or states, foods, cars, girls' names, etc.). Name four, three of which begin with the same letter, and one which begins with a different letter. Example: hippopotamus, hog, donkey, horse. Ask your child to tell you which animal's name does not begin with the same sound as the other three. Turn it around and let your child come up with four words for you, three of which must begin with the same sound. It is important to switch places when you play these games, so that your child isn't always on the receiving end of the game. He learns as much by having to construct questions for you. He also has to exercise his auditory memory in order to decide if your answer is right or wrong.

> Name three states, trees, flavors of ice cream or kinds of candy bars — whatever you feel like at the time.(For example: Texas, Rhode Island, Florida.) Tell your child that you are going to mix them up and say them again, only you're going to add another state this time. His job is to clap when he hears the new state. (Florida, Texas, Vermont -CLAP!- and hopefully, you won't even get to say "Rhode Island.")

> Find as many objects as possible which are made of different materials and will make distinctly different sounds when tapped. Have your child close his eyes and try to guess what material is being tapped. (For example: a glass, a can, a block of wood, a pie pan, a cardboard box, a book, etc.)

> Take a walk with your child and make a point of listening for as many different sounds as possible. Try to identify each.

Auditory Memory

> Read or say a sentence to your child and ask him to repeat it. Start with short sentences and build up to longer ones. Stop before your child becomes frustrated. End following a success!

This type of game can be played with an endless variety of lists to be repeated: numbers, names of friends, names of cartoon characters or rock musicians, and so on. You can also build a sentence: I swim. I swim quickly. I swim quickly and quietly. I swim in the cool water quickly and quietly.

> Play the game, "I'm Going on a Trip," where each person adds a new object to the list of things being taken. For example, the first person might say, "I'm going on a trip to Hawaii, and I'm taking a toothbrush." The second person would repeat the first sentence and

add to it. "I'm going on a trip and I'm taking a tooth-brush and a book." And so on.

➤ Have your child listen to a three- or four-minute news brief which most television stations air between regular programs. When it's over, ask him questions about the material reported. If your child has trouble with this, encourage him to jot down notes during the news brief. Let him use his notes to tell you all he can remember about the report after it's over.

➤ Learn songs by listening to them and singing them together.

Visual Discrimination

➤ Using interesting magazine photographs or book illus-trations, ask your child to look carefully and describe the pictures, noting colors, textures, categorizing things. Ask him to imitate the activity or pose of any people in the pictures.

➤ When you go shopping, give your child his own shop-ping list, with brand names and sizes listed. Have him search for his items.

➤ Look at a cereal box and find the word "Vitamins" or another which appears more than once on the box. Point it out to your child and ask him to find it written on another part of the box.

➤ Find a place where you can leave a good-size (but not overwhelmingly difficult) jigsaw puzzle undisturbed for a few days until it is finished. Help your child start, by together finding all the edge pieces and building the "frame."

Visual Memory

➤ On separate pieces of paper, write down three similar phone numbers. Point out one as being important ("It's Grandma's" or the number for the fire station). Then shuffle the pieces of paper and ask your child to pick out the important one.

➤ Show your child a picture of something that's of interest to him and ask him to look at it very carefully. Then turn the picture over and ask him questions about the picture. How many people in it? What were the people doing? What were they wearing? What color was the house? and so on.

➤ Draw a simple line design while your child watches. Erase or remove the picture and ask your child to duplicate it.

➤ On a table, place four objects. Have your child look at the objects and then turn around while you remove one of them. When he turns back, ask him to tell you which object you removed. Add more objects only if your child seems ready.

Following and Giving Directions

➤ Hide an object somewhere in the house or in a particular room. Write a set of directions telling where to start and how to find the object. Try this exercise, first allowing your child to take the paper with the directions with him. Later, try having him read the directions and then leave the paper with you and follow the instructions from memory. Reverse roles. Older children are challenged by writing instructions on how to pitch a baseball, tie a shoe, or cook an omelette.

➤ Draw a design (start with a simple one) on a piece of paper without letting your child see it. Give your child a blank piece of paper and orally direct him to reproduce the design. When you are through, compare the two pictures. Reverse roles.

➤ Write instructions similar to the ones below. Then either read them one at a time for your child to follow, or let him read and follow them.

★ Holding your paper vertically, draw a line from the top left corner to the bottom right corner.

★ Make a mark half-way along the line.

★ Connect the mark to the top right corner of the paper.

★ Draw a circle in the bottom left corner of the paper.

★ Write your phone number in the top left corner.

Working with your child, practice map skills using the map below. Take time to explain directions (north, east, south and west, northwest, southwest, and so on). Discuss words like diagonal and opposite, and explain how symbols and a key (or legend) are used.

Directions

★ Label N, S, E, and W along the sides of the map in the boxes. Point to the SE corner of the paper, the SW and so on.

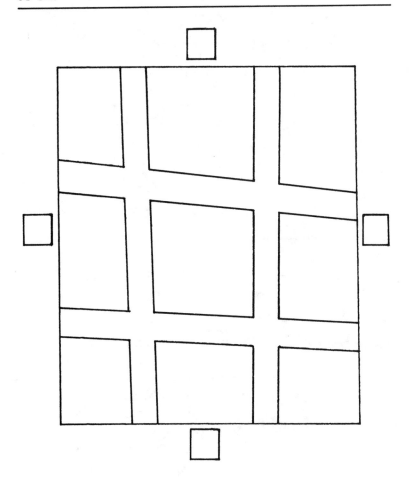

★ Label the westernmost North-South street "Slippery Street."

★ Label the easternmost North-South street "Active Avenue."

★ Label the northernmost East-West street "Bumpy Boulevard."

★ Label the southernmost East-West street "Radar Road."

★ Draw a church on the northwest corner of Bumpy Boulevard and Active Avenue.

★ Diagonally across from the church, draw a gas station.

★ On the south side of Radar Road, between Slippery Street and Active Avenue, draw a park.

★ Draw a river flowing east-west about half-way between Bumpy Boulevard and Radar Road. Give it a name.

★ Draw bridges over the river, along Slippery Street and Active Avenue.

★ Draw houses along both sides of Bumpy Boulevard, west of Slippery Street.

★ Draw a hospital south of Radar Road and east of Active Avenue.

You can create additional maps or use local maps and ask your child to follow oral or written instructions to go someplace.

Learning Problems

Before getting into the subject of learning problems, I'd like to offer a word of caution. Don't rush to label a child "learning disabled." It's important to remember that children mature physically, intellectually and emotionally at different rates. It is very possible that a child in first or even second grade who is not yet reading with ease may simply not be ready to read. Boys, in particular, seem to be slower in getting ready to deal with the skills involved in reading. Therefore, before jumping to the conclusion that your child is learning disabled, make an effort to ascertain that his problems are not simply due to overplacement or immaturity.

Even if you are quite sure there is some problem, don't rush to label it. The biggest problem with labels is that it's too easy for everyone — student, parent and teacher — to use the label or diagnosis as an excuse rather than an incentive.

With this said, I would like parents to be aware of a number of factors which can indeed cause learning problems. Some are physical in nature, some are psychological, and others involve the way an individual child's brain functions. It is the parent's job to watch for possible problems and to have his child evaluated by the appropriate professionals before he enters school, and then regularly throughout his school years.

Visual Problems

I t is important that a child's vision be professionally tested about the time he is ready to begin school and again every few years. Ask your pediatrician, school nurse, or friends to recommend a good opthamologist.

When a child enters school and is required to focus his eyes on the chalkboard, charts and books, problems involving the eyes' ability to focus may appear. Glasses may be required by a child with myopia (nearsightedness), hyperopia (farsightedness), or astigmatism. The sooner these conditions are diagnosed and treated, the less chance they will adversely affect the child's progress in school.

Hearing and Speech Problems

Loss of hearing can cause learning problems. The most common causes of hearing loss in preschool children are foreign objects in the ear, wax in the external ear, and middle-ear infections. Middle-ear infections often occur in older children as well.

Indications of a possible hearing problem include a child favoring one ear over the other, or not seeming to hear whispered words. Children with hearing problems may become anxious in noisy environments because they are having difficulty focusing on particular sounds. Other signs include noticeable changes in language and pronunciation, and a child who seems to ignore verbal requests or appears confused when asked simple questions. Because a hearing loss can occur at any time, parents should be sure their child's hearing is tested regularly.

Problems with speech may be related to a loss in hearing or to the inability of the brain to process language correctly. While certain mispronunciations may be "cute" in preschoolers, they may signal a more serious problem which can cause learning problems in school. Reasons for having a child's speech evaluated include problems in articulation (pronunciation), stuttering, a child's difficulty in expressing himself and general voice problems (volume, pitch, breathiness).

Parents who suspect their preschool child has a hearing or speech problem should contact a professional language-speech pathologist (your pediatrician can refer you to one). Parents of a school-age child with speech or hearing problems should speak with the head of the Special Education department at his school. These types of problems are treatable. Many schools offer free evaluations and treatment for speech problems. Overcoming them can tremendously improve a child's chances to read, write, and achieve his potential as a student.

Other Physical Causes of Learning Problems

There are a number of other physical conditions which can make learning difficult for a child, including hunger (a child who doesn't eat breakfast will have a hard time concentrating), allergies, hypoglycemia, Attention Deficit Disorder and hyperactivity. For this reason, a child who seems to have learning problems should have a complete physical.

Psychological Causes

Learning problems in children can be emotional. Stressful situations at home such as divorce, alcoholism, financial worries or moving to a new neighborhood, can all create stress for a child, as can the pressure to perform (especially in learning to read). Stress, whatever the cause, can make it next to impossible for a child to concentrate and learn. Parents need to determine the reasons for the child's stress, and work, possibly with counseling, to help the child deal with the situation in a healthy way.

Neuro-physiological Causes of Learning Problems

Other learning problems are more complex in nature and involve the way the individual's brain processes information. *Children with learning disabilities are often extremely bright;* it's very possible that a child's so-called disability is the result of a learning style which doesn't match the typically "left-brained curriculum" offered in most classrooms. It's vital that these children be provided instruction in their own learning style and taught alternative approaches to learning.

If you and your child's teacher determine that a discrepancy in learning and teaching styles is the cause for the child's problems, work to keep your child in his own classroom. Encourage his teacher to make some changes which will accommodate the child's individual learning style.

Sometimes the only one trained or willing to teach to different learning styles is the Special Education teacher. Confer with your child's classroom teacher and the Special Education teacher. Make it a team effort to determine how you can work together to best help your child. Try to keep your child in his classroom as much as possible.

Sometimes the cause of a child's learning problems is more than a mismatch of teaching and learning styles. Perceptual problems (visual or auditory) can make learning frustrating and difficult. In such situations, a parent's responsibility is to obtain special help for his child through the school.

Special Education: The Pros and Cons and How It Works

It is never easy for a parent to admit that his child has a problem. There is the worry that the child's ego will suffer if he goes to the Special Education classroom for help. Will his classmates tease? Possibly, but probably not for long. More important, how will your child's ego survive if he remains in his regular classroom, his problem untreated, and experiences repeated failure?

As a teacher, I know that a few students clearly need more individual and intense help than I can offer during a regular school day. I also am aware of how much a child misses academically and socially when he is away from the classroom. For these and other reasons, it is hard for parents to know whether or not to agree to special placement or remedial help for their child outside the regular classroom. Each individual situation must be scrutinized separately by all concerned in order to come up with the educational program which is best for the child in question.

Public Law 94-142 requires all states to provide an appropriate education for children with special learning problems. If you sense that your child is not progressing academically as he should, don't hesitate to speak with his teacher about the idea of having him tested to determine the cause of the problem. It is the responsibility of the school to provide any testing, although you may choose to seek independent professional advice on the matter.

If the school is the first to raise the question of a learning problem, you will be informed in writing and you must give your permission for testing. By law, the reasons for the referral, the results of the testing, and all proposed actions *must* be explained to you. (Don't be intimidated. Ask questions until you clearly understand.)

In either case, if tests reveal that a disability exists, an Individual Education Plan (IEP) will be developed for your child. You may question any part of the process, and you have the final say as to what type of program, if any, your child enters. The people involved in this assessment and IEP should try to develop a program which removes your child from his regular classroom environment as little as possible. Above all, remember that a child with learning problems needs his parents and his teacher to remain positive and supportive, dealing with the situation in a matter-of-fact way. ("Here's the problem. This is what we can do to solve it. I'll be here to help in any way I can.") Never lose sight of the fact that your child needs to believe that the problem can be overcome. He also needs to know you love him, learning problem and all.

Homework

Homework is one of those topics which seems to generate controversy. Opinions on homework differ from teacher to teacher, school to school, parent to parent. Only students tend to agree — they wouldn't mind if it had never been "invented."

There are a number of reasons for assigning homework. Most are valid, a few are not. The list which follows describes the most common types of worthwhile homework assignments:

★ Completion of work begun in class.

★ Reinforcement of a skill being learned in school.

★ "Extending" a skill learned in school. This type of assignment asks a child to do some creative thinking, solve a problem or give an opinion using information or applying techniques learned in the classroom.

★ Encouraging independent reading or creative projects.

★ Research. This may be a short or long assignment requiring the student to use any of a number of resources and report back his findings.

Unfortunately, children sometimes come home with assignments of questionable value. These include most fill-in-the-blank, "busywork" worksheets, and page after page of the same kind of math problem repeated over and over. Another type of poor assignment is one which is too vague or too broad and overwhelming, or one which requires the use of resources unavailable to some children.

If the majority of your child's assignments are questionable, make an appointment to speak to his teacher about it. You are certainly within your rights as a parent to ask her to explain her philosophy on homework, or the purpose of a particular assignment. Approach her with your concerns and diplomatically offer suggestions for more creative assignments.

Helping with Homework

Some will say that homework is the child's responsibility entirely, and that parents should not get involved. To me, this attitude fails to recognize the role parents play in education. A child's success in school must be a cooperative, team effort, with the child, the parents, and the teacher involved.

Obviously, a parent should not do the child's assignment. This would only deprive the child of an opportunity to learn. However, a parent should be available to explain things and get the child headed in the right direction if asked. *When you consider that homework should be an experience in learning — not an experience in frustration — the framework for helping your child becomes clearer.* In addition, homework is an ideal opportunity to share interest and excitement about learning, to show your child that you don't know all the answers ("I don't know the answer. Let's try to figure it out together."), and to be supportive ("That is a lot of math. I'll sit down in here and balance the checkbook while you finish up. Then we'll have some ice cream").

Parents may need to help in scheduling homework time. If a child seems lost as to where to begin, help him before he decides not to begin at all. Sit down and talk about his alternatives. He can begin with the toughest assignment and get it out of the way first, or he might prefer getting the easier and quicker assignments taken care of before settling down to the one which will require the most concentration. Help him decide which feels best to him.

Then have him jot down the assignments in the order he decides upon. As each is completed, he should check it off. This will allow him to see his progress and experience a sense of accomplishment.

Children should have some say about when to do their homework. Once you and your child decide upon a time for homework, it should become a regular part of the daily routine. The sooner your child establishes a consistent schedule for doing homework, the less of a chore it will be.

Miscellaneous Homework Tips

★ With some assignments, such as spelling tests, which occur regularly, it may be helpful for your child to study 5 words each night for 4 nights, rather than try to learn all 20 in one night.

★ Help your child find a place where he can set his books when he's finished with his homework — preferably near the door he uses on his way out of the house in the morning.

★ If your child repeatedly has his homework "run over" into his bedtime or later, help him rethink his schedule. Does he need to begin earlier? Does he waste time while supposedly on task? Does he actually have too much to do?

★ If your child forgets a homework assignment or a book at home, and calls to ask you to bring it to school for him, do him a favor and don't. Tell him, "I'm sorry. Remembering your homework is your responsibility. I'm afraid you'll have to suffer the consequences." As hard-hearted as this may sound, it's the most effective way for him to learn a very important lesson.

★ If you are expected to quiz your child for a test, make sure it is done to suit your schedule, and not left until the last moment.

CHAPTER
THREE

The Joy of Reading

THREE

The Joy of Reading

Far back in my memory, I hear my father reading to me the story of *The Little Red Hen*. "'Then I'll do it myself,' said the Little Red Hen. And she did." Why I remember that particular story or those particular words, I don't know, but there they remain.

Another important book-related memory is from the second-grade when Mrs. Amren read *Charlotte's Web* to my class. What I remember most are the different voices that she used for the characters, making the book come alive. It was like magic!

By the time I was in junior high, books were so welcome a part of my life that I would sometimes, on a Sunday afternoon, take a book to the pasture where my horse grazed. I would climb up and sit, backwards, book resting on my horse's rump, and read as she walked around, grazing contentedly.

Today, with a 5-year-old and never enough time, I don't get to read for my own pure enjoyment as much as I'd like. Most of what I read is what I read aloud to my son. I particularly enjoy giving each character his own voice, trying to do for my son what was done for me when I was young.

One of the greatest gifts parents can give their children is a love of books — because being able to read well dramatically increases a person's opportunities for success and pleasure in life.

The Value of Reading Aloud

The bedtime story is perhaps the favorite read-aloud format. It is a pleasant, relaxing way to end the day. It also creates for both the parent and the child, a special sense of something shared —

laughter, sadness, surprise, wonder, excitement at new places "visited." Stretch out on your child's bed, your arm around him as you hold the book so you can both see it, and lose yourself in the story for the time you spend reading together. But, don't limit yourselves to sitting on a bed or couch. Try sitting on the porch, in a tent, on a blanket in the back yard, or up in a tree. During a nice rain, take a few books and a snack and read in the car. (Be sure it's parked where the rain drums nicely on the roof.) Use your imagination to find new places, new excuses for combining reading and fun.

Reading aloud to your child provides him with the opportunity to exercise his imagination. Take time to help your child visualize what he reads. Teach him how to picture characters or scenes in his mind by sharing the pictures you have in your own mind. Practice by asking him to close his eyes and imagine, say, a monster. Ask him questions which invite him to develop a more elaborate image than the word "monster" provides. "How big is the monster?" "What color is it?" "How many teeth does it have?" "Is it a hairy monster or a slimy one?" Try the same from time to time as you read books together. Ask your child to close his eyes and imagine what a certain character's home or family or pet looks like. "How do you see him now? Is he lying on his back or his stomach?" "Does his mother look angry or sad?"

Along with the opportunity to create images, books offer the chance to get emotionally "into a story." Encourage your child to put himself in the place of a particular character and "try on" how it feels to be in that character's situation. Take advantage of the opportunities that books present for discussing ideas, values and resolving problems. Listen to your child's thoughts first; if appropriate, offer your own ideas without asking or expecting your child to adopt them as his own.

Help your child realize that reading involves far more than recognizing printed words. To enjoy reading, he must become an active participant, for therein lies the greatest joy.

Choosing the Right Books

I t's important to choose books which match a child's interests, especially once he has begun to read. In addition to increasing his enthusiasm for reading, books which are appealing in content may challenge him to read more difficult books on a particular subject. As a result, his vocabulary expands and his reading skills improve.

Reading aloud and appropriate literature for children are hot topics now, as well they should be. I'd like to mention several books which I think are worth checking out of the library or buying. They can help you choose books which your child is most likely to enjoy. Both *The Read-Aloud Handbook*, by Jim Trelease, and *Books Kids Will Sit Still For*, by Judy Freeman, encourage parents to read aloud to their children, even through elementary school, and describe hundreds of books to consider. A third is Nancy Larrick's *A Parent's Guide to Children's Reading*, which describes and lists books for children to read themselves. All three also offer many ideas to encourage reading.

No matter how carefully you choose a book, from time to time you may find yourself reading a book to your child which turns out to be boring or which neither of you cares for. When this happens, abandon the book and start something else. The whole point of reading with your child is enjoyment.

How to Sell Your Child on Books

I n this age of telecommunications, parents need to "sell" their children on books and reading. By simply reading themselves, parents tell their children that reading is a worthwhile and pleasurable use of time. Having an abundance and variety of reading material in the home also tells the child that reading is important. In addition to books, there should be newspapers, magazines, catalogues, even comic books! Talk about what you are reading now and share favorite book memories.

Try to develop a home library. This can be done with new books from bookstores, used books from yard sales and discards from libraries. Many schools hold used book sales where kids can buy books for 5 cents or 10 cents. School book clubs offer a wonderful way to purchase books inexpensively. They offer new publications as well as old favorites. It is always exciting for my classes when a shipment of books arrives. It is a wonderful treat for those who ordered books. I also always buy a few books to add to the class library. I make a point of holding up each book and reading its back cover as a way of introducing it, "selling" it to the class. Few books, if any, make it to the shelf.

A valuable addition to a home library is a junior set of encyclopedias. This is especially important for children in the upper elementary grades. Like anything else, some sets are better than others. According to Nancy Larrick, teachers and librarians most widely recommend the following: *Compton's Encyclopedia*, *World Book Encyclopedia*, and *The New Book of Knowledge* (Grolier).

You may want to subscribe to a magazine for your child. There are numerous publications which offer stories, puzzles and worthwhile information appropriate for different age levels. We all love to get mail, and receiving magazines in the mail links reading with something exciting. Book clubs do the same thing, but they tend to be a more costly investment.

Learning to Read

My son, Nathan, has always loved books. When he was 2, I must have read *The Little Red Caboose* to him several hundred times before we moved onto the next favorite. I consider the development of this enjoyment of books my son's first step on the road to reading.

At age 3, Nathan was not a reader, but he understood that letters represented words, and words represented things. This is the second step a child takes in becoming a reader.

One day, when he was 4, Nathan surprised me when he looked at a jar of grape jelly I'd just bought at the store.

"Is that mayonnaise?" he asked.

"No, sweetheart," I said, slightly puzzled by his mistake. "That's jelly."

"It looks like mayonnaise," he explained as he pointed to the word "KRAFT" on the jar.

Then it hit me. It was indeed the same word that he'd seen on the jar of mayonnaise in the refrigerator! Not such a strange mistake after all! I let him know that I thought he was terribly observant to have noticed the word on both jars. On subsequent occasions, he correctly identified the brand name, KRAFT, without hesitation.

This sort of word recognition which precedes or accompanies individual letter recognition is the third important step in learning to read. It should also tell us something: While for most adults, phonics is an important part of reading, children often begin to learn to read on their own by association of whole words to objects. The challenge of recognizing words is a game, and should be great fun for all.

It is important not to rush at this point. *We cannot push a child into the next stage.* A parent should, instead, take advantage of his child's natural interest in words to help the child build up a sizable sight vocabulary. Introduce words that are meaningful emotionally (for example, the names of brothers, sisters and friends, "Mom," "Dad," the names of pets, "car," "bike," "fast," "zoom!"), or words the child hears and uses frequently ("the," "friend," "Hi," "please," "yes," "no"). It will help at the next stage if some of the words your child learns now by sight are spelled phonetically (words like "Mom," "cat," "like," "me"). This way, they can be used later to show how to sound out words.

Watch for clues indicating the child is ready to move on. The reason for such caution is that at the next stage learning to read becomes more difficult, as the child is introduced to phonics and the skills needed to decode. In phonics, he learns what letter makes what sound. He learns what makes words look and sound as they do, so that eventually he will be able to decipher unfamiliar words independently.

Learning to Decode

The best indication of readiness to learn phonics is a child's own interest in the letters of the alphabet. He will ask, "What's this letter?" and want to learn to write his name and other words. If the child is not yet in school and expresses a serious interest in learning to read, the parent can begin to teach the basic skills of decoding or phonics.

If the child is already in school, his teacher should be introducing the same decoding skills, although how much emphasis is placed on phonics will depend on the method she is using to teach reading. It is best for parents to find out and use the same sequence that the teacher is using, so that the child senses order in learning, not confusion.

Parental involvement at this stage helps children maintain a positive attitude toward learning to read. Though the task of learning to decode is not easy, it can be fun! Parents can play games with their children and can make an effort to find especially fun books to read aloud, reinforcing the reason for learning this difficult skill.

Reading materials for the beginning reader focus on learning to relate print to speech. Therefore, few new words or ideas are introduced. Once a child has learned to confidently decode words (generally in grades two and three), he becomes a faster and more fluent reader. During this stage it becomes increasingly clear that the more varied the child's experiences and the greater his vocabulary, the easier it is for him to read new words. Library books should be used to supplement the basal reader used in school, so that the richness and variety of reading is always unfolding for each child.

Reading to Learn

Fluency, the ability to read with ease and confidence, is necessary before children can succeed at the next stage, using reading as a tool to master new knowledge and ideas. Reading to learn now supplants learning to read. This stage usually begins in fourth grade, where more formal texts in subjects such as science and social studies are introduced, and the uses of reading are more demanding. For this reason, parents of fourth graders shouldn't be surprised to witness a slump in their child's grades. Continued support and help are important here. Help is especially needed in recognizing new words in science and social studies and discussing the concepts these words name. A child needs to be able to picture what happens in "evaporation" or "revolution." It is not enough to recognize and say the words.

From this point on, reading involves learning to comprehend increasingly difficult reading materials and to analyze critically the varying viewpoints presented by different authors. Reading gradually competes more and more with listening and watching as a means of gaining information. Silent reading becomes preferable to reading aloud, as it is a more effective way to comprehend meaning and a more efficient use of study time.

Methods Used in Teaching Reading

There are different approaches to teaching reading: programs which stress phonics, where letters are assigned sounds and a child learns to sound out words while reading in basal readers; a language experience approach where a child learns to read stories he has dictated to the teacher; a whole-language approach, which ties together listening, speaking, writing and reading as integral parts of a language program. Most reading programs found in schools today involve a combination of approaches differing in when and where the major emphasis is placed.

There are things which parents can do to help their children learn more easily. The following activities should not interfere with any reading program your child is involved in at school. You may want to check with your child's teacher about the reading program she is following and describe the kinds of activities you would like to offer your child. The only prerequisite to these activities is that your child recognize the letters of the alphabet. He may or may not know the sound each makes. That's where phonics come in.

Phonics

No matter how many words we learn to recognize by sight, there will always be words which cause us to hesitate in our reading. These are words which require dissection in order for us to simply pronounce them. This activity involves decoding or phonics. The main point to keep in mind is that *phonics should be considered a tool, not a teaching method by itself. It will only help one pronounce. Reading — getting meaning out of words — involves far more than the pronunciation of groups of letters.*

Many children learn to read most easily by using the step-by-step, building block approach supplied by phonics. These children have brains which function logically. They are the ones who have more difficulty learning to read if taught by another method. Phonics will help them decipher words and get them started, but there are many other skills they need to master in order to become proficient readers.

Inconsistent and frustrating as our language can be, phonics does have rules which work pretty well most of the time. My first book, *Parents Are Teachers, Too,* explains the basic rules of phonics and suggests activities for parents to use in teaching the rules to their children. There are also numerous workbooks available which explain the rules of phonics and offer activities.

While no two authorities totally agree on when and how to teach phonics, the prerequisites seem to be clear: good speech and oral vocabulary, good visual and auditory discrimination (the ability to distinguish one letter from another and one sound from another), recognition of the letters of the alphabet, and good hand control for writing.

Phonics Activities

Note: Take care to go slowly in teaching phonics. Follow the sequence being taught in school, and play lots of games to reinforce a single letter sound before introducing a new one. Then be sure to continually review old sounds along with the new.

➤ Make a set of letter cards by writing individual letters of the alphabet on index cards. (Make at least two of each consonant, and three or four of each vowel — a,e,i,o,u.) Use these cards to reinforce each new letter sound your child learns. For example:

★ Say a word and have your child pick out from several cards, the letter whose sound is heard at the beginning of that word. (This same game can be played for ending sounds.)

★ Hold up one letter card at a time. Let your child "win" each card for which he can think of a word beginning (or ending) with that letter.

★ Using the letter cards, spell out two words and have your child point to the word you say.

★ Ask or help your child to make words using the letter cards for those sounds he already knows.

★ Point to objects or pictures and ask your child to tell or write the beginning sound or letter.

★ Play a game of initials of people you both know. "Who is P.G.?"

The Language Experience Approach

The language experience approach to reading instruction involves a child dictating his own real experiences, dreams or stories to his teacher, who writes them down on large chart paper or in storybook form. The child then learns to read stories which hold meaning for him by reading his own words.

In order for this type of language experience approach to be most effective, it needs to be combined with discussion about the story and activities which teach phonics, cause and effect, and so on.

Language Experience Activity

➤ Offer to write down stories your child dictates, and suggest that he practice reading them to others in the family. He may want to illustrate them as well. As soon as he is capable of writing simple words, encourage him to try writing the stories by himself. It's important that you don't correct his spelling at this point. Spelling will improve with time and practice. If he asks you to spell a word for him, you can help him sound it out, but don't make it a long, drawn-out chore or he won't want to write any more. Often it's best to simply tell him the correct spelling so that he can continue writing. Encourage your child to read his stories to you more than once. The repetition will help him develop fluency and thus, confidence.

Using the Whole-Language Approach

A relatively new and encouraging approach to reading is called the whole-language approach. The main idea behind this approach is that the more a child uses language (in speech, listening, writing and reading), the better he becomes at the skills involved. This goes along with the idea that learning to read is like learning to talk; at first a child will approximate adult language, and the more he practices, the more accurate he will become. In whole-language teaching, all areas of language are tied to the thinking process.

Whole-language also emphasizes the "inside-out" nature of reading, the idea that what a child brings to reading influences how much he gets out of it. Therefore, the more reading is tied to things the child knows and experiences, and the greater the variety of experiences he has, the easier it is for him to learn to read.

In the whole-language classroom, children are surrounded by good literature and are read to every day. They are encouraged to take risks as they read themselves. For instance, if a child comes across a word he doesn't know, he might look at the first letter and guess, or simply skip it. The idea is that after a few sentences, he can probably go back and guess the word. In this way, the child is allowed to "experiment" as he learns to read. He is not corrected too quickly or too often, but rather learns to correct himself. The whole-language approach trusts the child to know how to learn, using the feedback he gets as he reads. If he sees that a word he guessed doesn't make sense, he will go back and try again.

In the same way, whole-language classrooms encourage "inventive spelling." When writing stories, it is considered far more important that a child write freely with mistakes than that he write unimaginative but accurate sentences. Spelling is corrected later during the editing process. Children are invited to correct and recopy their work and have books "published" for others to read.

Whole-Language Activities

➤ Read books together. You read one paragraph and your child reads the next, or you read a page and your child reads one. Be prepared to re-read the same book many times. Repetition builds confidence.

➤ Consider reading to your child and a friend who comes over to play. You might offer to read to them a little from a wonderful book you just found, and then suggest they continue on their own, taking turns reading to each other. They might want to take the book, along with a snack, up into a tree or to a home-made blanket tent. You can make the idea of reading an enticing one!

➤ To reinforce comprehension, help your child act out a story he has just read. Ask him to show you a particular character's walk or facial expressions. Encourage him to explain why a particular character behaved the way he did. Could he have behaved differently? Discuss the feelings exhibited by the characters. Encourage him to retell the story to another family member, paying attention to sequence of events.

Working with the Beginning Reader

In addition to reading good literature to his child, a parent can help a beginning reader by providing him with lots of books written just for him. Books like Dr. Seuss' *Hop On Pop* and *One Fish, Two Fish, Red Fish, Blue Fish* offer a helpful repetition of words in amusing contexts. Other good books for beginning readers include *Frog and Toad Are Friends*, and *Mouse Tales*, by Arnold Lobel; Norman Bridwell's *Clifford* books; *Albert the Albatross*, by Syd Hoff; and *Are You My Mother?* by P.D. Eastman. The

Frances books and *Little Bear* books by Russell Hoban are also geared to this stage.

Read the books to your child first, pointing to the words as you say them. The next time you read, stop occasionally, point to the next word and let your child say it from memory. He will be learning to associate the word he knows to the one he sees.

Reading Problems

A number of factors influence a child's readiness or ability to learn to read. Although children follow the same basic sequence in learning reading skills, the age at which they learn them varies from child to child. Consequently, it is important that parents not become overly anxious about a child who is not yet reading. At the same time, parents also need to recognize when to seek professional assessment of the situation.

Parents who must move to a new location during their child's first three or four years of school should inform each new teacher what reading system or methods were used in the previous schools. Children who have moved a lot during these early school years may need short-term tutoring or reading help, not evaluation for a disability.

In order to develop realistic expectations, parents should have a rough idea of when children begin learning to read. According to Dorothy Cohen, author of *The Learning Child*, most children are ready to learn the skills of decoding around the age of 7 years, or the end of first grade. However, these skills are now taught in kindergarten and the early part of first grade nationwide, possibly creating problems. Certainly there are those children who enter school already knowing how to read, but they are the minority.

A child who is quiet and not easily distracted may choose to sit and learn to read at a relatively early age, while a child who is more socially-oriented will focus his attention on developing friendships during his early school years. A child who is strongly interested in developing new physical skills will find participating in sports and physical activities more desirable than sitting down to learn to read. Some children simply mature more quickly than others. Girls, in particular, seem to be ready to begin reading at an earlier age than boys, although by the time they reach fourth grade, many boys have caught up in reading achievement.

All of this should tell us to give a child a little time before we start to worry. More than anything a child who is slow to read needs to be reassured by his parents that they have confidence in his ability to learn to read. Patience and constant encouragement are critical if the child is to maintain a positive self-image and avoid feeling he has disappointed his parents or teacher. The fear of failure and disappointing one's parents can be a very real stumbling block to a child's learning to read.

If, by the middle of second grade, a child has not begun to learn the skills involved in reading, his parent probably has a legitimate reason to be concerned. At this point, the parent needs to seek the help of professionals in identifying if there is a problem and what steps to take for correction.

Potential Problems

There are a number of possible reasons for a child having difficulty learning to read. The following possible causes of a learning problem should be considered:

Poor vision: A child who has trouble reading should have his eyes tested by an optometrist or opthalmologist. Don't rely on the results of a routine school eye exam which tests only far vision. Large, scrawling handwriting may also be an indication of a vision problem.

Physical problems: In addition to vision and hearing problems, there are other physical conditions to consider when a child has trouble learning. These include a variety of allergies and hypoglycemia. A child who appears listless or pale may be hungry or suffer from lead-paint poisoning.

Neuro-physiological problems: Perceptual problems are involved in disabilities such as dyslexia, although many feel that educators are too quick to label children dyslexic or learning disabled when in fact many outgrow perceptual problems. (There are studies which estimate that in 1987, 1 child in 1,000 was truly dyslexic. If there are far more children labeled dyslexic in your child's school than this statistic would indicate, chances are the diagnoses are inaccurate. *Only a neurologist is qualified to diagnose a person as dyslexic.*)

Parents should be aware that it is normal for a child to occasionally reverse some letters or see them upside down or sideways. It is also not uncommon for a child to confuse "b" and "d", or "was" and "saw." These are reasonable mistakes made by someone learning something new! If this kind of tendency toward reversals persists beyond second grade, however, it is fair to investigate a possible neurological problem. Another indicator of a perceptual problem is when a child, sounding out a new word, consistently begins to read the word backwards. A third clue to a problem would be a child's inability to reproduce fairly accurately, a simple geometric shape, such as a diamond or circle. By the age of 6 1/2 or 7, a child should connect the four lines of a diamond at its corners, and close a circle.

Although neuro-physiological problems make learning to read much more difficult, in most cases, once the specific problem is identified, the child will be able to learn how to read.

Lack of motivation: A child who grows up in a household which places no real value on reading, may see no reason to learn to read. Chances are since you are reading this book, this will not apply to your child.

A mismatch of teaching and learning styles: Instructed by an effective teacher, the majority of children will learn to read regardless of the teaching method. It is possible, however, that for some children, one method will prove far more effective than another. Keep in mind the following:

★ **An auditory learner** should be taught through phonics. Materials used should include read-along cassette tapes. An older child who has had trouble learning to read will have to unlearn some bad habits before he can easily use phonics. It is important that he approach learning to read with logic. For him, guessing is not helpful.

★ **A visual learner** learns best through a whole-language approach where recognition of words by sight is stressed.

★ **A tactual learner** needs many experiences involving touch. (All 5- and 6-year-olds are concrete thinkers, but some are more so than others.) Tactual experiences include tracing words in sand; writing on a chalkboard with chalk or water and on paper with a variety of writing tools; molding words with clay; forming words with alphabet macaroni. Board games also work well for the tactual learner.

★ **A kinesthetic learner** should try walking back and forth while reading. He needs to see and use words in an activity which involves doing, such as baking cookies and focusing on words in the recipe, or building something and focusing on the words in the instructions. Writing on a chalkboard is both helpful and satisfying.

One last point to remember: Poor readers tend to perform better when working in dim light.

Emotional problems: There are many reasons for emotional problems, any of which may make it extremely difficult for a child to learn to read. They are also the most difficult problems to overcome.

A stressful situation at home can make it nearly impossible for a child to concentrate on learning. Feeling pressured to learn to read before he is ready can also create a great deal of stress in a child. In addition to worrying about disappointing his parents, he may have a hard time not living up to the high expectations he has for himself. Such pressure is especially difficult for a child for whom learning most skills has been easy, but whose efforts at reading have not resulted in such quick success. Body language can offer clues to a child who is feeling extremely anxious. Anxiousness distorts our visual perception so that we don't "see straight." We walk into the exit or read poorly, especially out loud.

If your child exhibits signs of anxiety over learning to read, help him to relax. You need to remind him that you expect him to make mistakes. Recount for him some of the mistakes he and everyone else made in learning to speak. You didn't mind him saying "sgetti" before he was capable of pronouncing "spaghetti." You knew he'd eventually get it right. The same is true for his learning to read.

Parents should not tutor a child who is highly anxious about reading, because he will be extra sensitive to any worry or impatience in the parent. He wants more than anything to please his parents. This child should get reading help at school, and nothing but encouragement from his parents and praise in his strengths.

Whatever the reason for a child's delayed reading, the parent's job is to do whatever is necessary to see that a professional diagnosis is completed and a suitable program developed as quickly and effectively as possible.

Working with the More Advanced Reader

As reading abilities progress, children experience a welcome feeling of independence. Reading becomes much more enjoyable. If the child can find books to read which are of interest, and easy enough without being too simple, chances are good that he will become a steady reader.

Like it or not, television has done a great deal to accelerate the rate at which children mature. By fifth and sixth grades, many children are looking for books concerning topics once reserved for adults. In response to the changing times, and in answer to the questions and needs of preteens today, books are written which deal with such topics as divorce, drug abuse, alcoholism, rape, abortion, disabilities and homosexuality. There are also many adventure, mystery and humorous books, as well as biographies available. Many children also devour informational books on sports, hobbies, and animals. And there are old favorites whose popularity never seems to diminish.

I encourage parents to continue with bedtime stories for as long as possible. There are absolutely wonderful books to read to upper elementary children. Despite an older child's occasional objections to "parental guidance," he still needs your attention and affection. He needs hugs and reassurance that you haven't abandoned him to a world that can be rather frightening at times. He wants to be reminded about what is right and what is wrong. Books offer the opportunity to discuss some confusing issues without getting too personal. Talking about a character's dilemmas, choices and decisions allows a child to consider his own values.

If a child really doesn't want to listen to his parent read aloud to him, an alternative would be for both to read the same book and informally talk about it, a chapter at a time.

Activities Which Encourage Reading

➤ Record albums often include the words to songs. This is another reason for an older child to read if he happens to like a particular singer or group.

➤ Let your child tape record and listen to himself reading. It is fascinating to hear oneself on tape, and it is an objective way for a child to decide where he needs to improve.

➤ Comic strips and comic books provide wonderful opportunities to reinforce the skills your child is learning in school.

➤ To review punctuation, ask your child to highlight or circle all periods, commas and so on in his favorite comic strip and explain why each has been used.

➤ On one page of a comic book, your child might look for prefixes (or suffixes). Ask him what each means and what the root word is.

➤ Find antonyms on a page in a comic book. List the "other halves" to the antonyms. For instance, if the word "angry" is on the page, you could write "happy." (The same activity could be done with synonyms.)

➤ Encourage your child to keep a running list of onomatopoeias he finds in the comics. These are sound words like "Blam!" "Screech!" "Boink!" and add fun to reading.

➤ After reading a comic book story together, ask your child who is the major character, and who are the minor characters. Can he describe each with an adjective or two?

➤ Older children might enjoy taking a book they've read and drawing and writing their own "comic book edition."

Using Context Clues

Beyond basic word recognition and phonics skills, are comprehension skills — learning to get meaning from words. Without meaning, reading is a lot of wasted effort.

If a child doesn't recognize and can't easily sound out a word, his chances of understanding that word are almost nil. Instead of giving up on a strange word, however, a child can learn to make an educated guess as to its meaning, by using context clues. Let's say, for instance, that your child is reading this sentence:

When the argument was over, both children were in tears.

Let's also say that your child doesn't recognize the word "argument." If he stops on the word, struggling to figure it out, he will lose the meaning of the sentence. Instead, he should continue reading, skipping the unknown word, but picking up from the context that something was upsetting to the children. At this point, your child can attack the word phonetically again with an increased chance of figuring it out. If he still can't decipher the word, he at least has an idea as to its meaning, and can continue reading. Later, he should get help with the word. The same can be done when a reader doesn't understand a particular sentence. Continue on and finish the paragraph. He will usually then grasp the meaning which originally escaped him.

Learning to use context clues is a major factor in determining how well a child comprehends what he reads. The ability to use context clues also gives a child confidence that "I can do something to solve the problems I run into."

Context Clue Activities

➤ Using a children's magazine or other reading material at the appropriate reading level, cross out with a heavy black marker, every sixth or eighth word. Have your child read the story to you, and using context clues, decide what those words are that you crossed out.

➤ Explain how context often determines the meaning of a word or phrase. For example, until you hear the rest of the sentence, you don't know what the word "run" means. Consider "I have a run in my stocking." "I like to run half a mile a day." "The boy wanted to learn how to run the machine." "He's going to run in the election."

➤ Discuss what it means when something is "taken out of context."

> Ask your child to use context clues to help him choose the correct meaning for the italicized words in the sentences below. Have him explain why he chose the word he did.

★ The president's speech was so *tedious* that most of the people in the audience fell asleep.

funny   **dull**   **short**

★ That mosquito's *aggravating* buzz is getting on my nerves.

annoying   **pleasant**   **quiet**

★ The rat's sharp teeth *gnawed* through the rope.

mended   **clicked**   **chewed**

★ Practice is *essential* to being a good tennis player.

simple   **necessary**   **unimportant**

★ Watch the stairs as you *descend* to the cellar.

go down   **climb**   **carry**

Using the Dictionary

"**W**hat's this word?" asks your daughter. You look over her shoulder to the word she is pointing to and provide the answer, "Barnacle."

"What's a barnacle?" she pursues.

Obligingly, you consider for a moment and answer, "It's like a little shell with an animal inside, that lives on rocks at the seashore, or on the bottom of boats. Some even live on whales."

In the example above, chances are even context clues would not have helped your child understand the word "barnacle." If your child is engrossed in a story, it's best to supply the answer and let him continue his reading. In other situations, this is when you steer the child to a dictionary.

A valuable habit to help your child develop is that of using a dictionary or a glossary in the back of a book when he runs across a word he doesn't know. Keep a dictionary handy, preferably one at the appropriate reading level for your child.

Point out that each word is respelled in parentheses immediately following the word, to show its pronunciation. Help your child learn to use the pronunciation key found at the bottom of each page. Explain how to use the guide words at the top of each page.

Dictionary Activities

➤ To help with alphabetizing skills, make some flash cards with words for him to arrange in alphabetical order on the table or floor. Start with words whose first letters are different: horse, boat, song. When he can arrange them easily in order, add words which have the same first letter: stop, sit, smell. Help your child learn to look at the second letter when necessary, or even the third: truck, train, tree; or fourth: place, play, plate. Actually having cards to manipulate and put in order helps many children understand the process of organization involved in alphabetizing.

➤ Ask your child to look up the word "train." Ask him which meaning given would best apply in the sentence: The bride's train was ten feet long. Now, take turns selecting other words and finding meanings appropriate to sentences.

➤ To provide practice in using the dictionary, you can easily come up with questions like the following for him to answer. Try to find interesting or amusing words.

★ If someone gave you a *fedora*, where would you wear it?

★ Is a *pickerel* a freshwater or saltwater fish?

★ *Sodium chloride* is usually called _____.

★ Where do the *Maori* people live?

★ How does a *python* kill its prey?

★ A *titmouse* is not a bird. It's a _____.

★ How many masts does a *yawl* have?

> Using two dictionaries, two children can have dictionary races. You say a word, and see who can locate it first.

> Make a dictionary page, by writing guide words at the top of a blank sheet of paper. Ask your child to cut out of the newspaper or a magazine, 5 words which would fit on that page, and glue them in the correct order.

Understanding Content Activities

Reading comprehension involves a number of important, individual skills. The activities listed below offer a parent a way to help his child develop them.

Main Idea Activities

> Talk about a show, picture or story. Make up a title for it. (A good title hints at or tells the point of the story.)

> Help your child make a scrapbook of some sort and encourage him to label the pages with headings and subheadings that state major ideas or themes.

> With an older child, ask for the main idea of a paragraph in a book.

Sequencing Activities

> A child should be able to remember, arrange and tell in order, the main events of a story. The main events are the ones that involve causes and effects in the story.

> Make a timeline or booklet to show the sequence of the events in a "normal" day. Discuss which events cause other events to happen.

> Choose a particularly funny comic strip, cut it out and cut apart the individual boxes. Mix them up and ask your child to rearrange the boxes in the correct order.

➤ Talk with your child about stories you have read together, or movies you've seen. Encourage him to describe them to other family members. You may have to prompt him with, "How did it start?" and "What happened next?" Be sure he understands and uses correctly, words involved in time and sequencing such as: next, last, then, finally, now, first, soon, tomorrow, yesterday, past, present, future.

Drawing Conclusions Activities

➤ A child can learn to read "clues," anticipate results and recognize the relationship of cause and effect. This skill of drawing conclusions will be useful in far more areas than reading. As you read a story together, ask, "What do you think will happen next?" Have your child explain his logic and the clues he is using.

➤ Read fables and ask your child to try and figure out the morals.

➤ Make a game of providing beginnings to sentences and having your child supply appropriate endings. ("I am tired because..." or "I am going to the store because..." or "Loren's fingers are purple because...")

➤ Look for books in the *Encyclopedia Brown* series, which include short mysteries for the reader to solve. Read them together and make a game of watching for clues.

Critical Thinking Activities

➤ Ask your child if a movie is fiction or non-fiction. What about news on T.V.? Help him understand the difference between the two. Consider the various reading materials around your house. Is the information true (non-fiction) or just a story (fiction)?

➤ Discuss *fact versus opinion*. What makes something fact rather than opinion? Ask your child whether the following statements are fact or opinion:

| ★ Water boils at 32 degrees F. or 0 degrees C. |
| ★ Horses are beautiful animals. |
| ★ Spring is the best season of the year. |
| ★ Florida is the southernmost state in the United States. |
| (These are pretty obvious examples, useful in explaining the concepts. Make an effort to find less obvious statements of fact and opinion to talk about with your child. This is especially pertinent to reading the newspaper.) |

➤ Talk with your child about the *concept of propaganda.* Use commercials and advertisements in magazines as examples. How do companies try to get you to buy their product rather than another? What is political propaganda?

➤ Discuss issues that come up in the news and at home. Help your child look at both sides of an argument. You will open his mind to differing opinions and alternatives to a problem or issue. Ask him to describe the steps in his thinking that led to his conclusion or decision. This way, he will learn to inquire, find evidence and make thoughtful conclusions, instead of following others or making hasty guesses.

Using the Telephone Directory

I f someone in your family fell and was unconscious, would your youngster know how to call for emergency help? Could he dial the correct number, describe the situation and give a complete address? Hopefully this particular skill will never have to be tested, but every child should know how to get emergency help.

Telephone skills and using the telephone directory are both useful and important in emergency situations, and for information gathering as well. The phone book can be a way to introduce your child to research skills and allow him to practice them. He will see a reason for learning to put things in alphabetical order. He will also become familiar with the process of "digging for information," making future research efforts in other areas that much easier.

Below are some more questions to help your child become familiar with the telephone directory.

Directory Activities

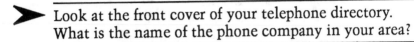 Look at the front cover of your telephone directory. What is the name of the phone company in your area?

What cities does it cover?

What is the area code for your city or town?

Look inside the front cover. What is the number to call if a fire started in your house?

What number would you call to get the police?

If your mother fell and broke her leg, what number would you call to get an ambulance?

Look through some of the Yellow Pages. What are they for?

Look in the Yellow Pages under SCHOOLS. Find the phone number for the school you attend.

On one of the first few Yellow Pages you should find a list of zip codes. Find the zip code for your town.

How are names listed in a phone book?

Can you find your best friend's phone number.

If you needed your bike repaired, would you look in the White Pages or the Yellow pages for a repair shop? Which repair shop would you take your bike to?

Newspaper Activities

Any school-age child can begin to learn what's inside those rustling sheets of newsprint. The better his reading skills, the more of the following questions he will be able to answer. Help your child learn to use the newspaper as a tool.

➤ What is the name of the newspaper? How many sections are there in today's paper? What is the biggest news story (headline) about? Using the index, on what page will you look to find the comics? T.V. listings? sports? local news?

➤ Find the weather information and answer the following: What is the expected high temperature today for the area in which you live? How cold is it expected to get tonight in your area? What was the low temperature for Fairbanks, Alaska?

➤ Find the comics and read them all. Which is your favorite? Who is the creator of your favorite strip?

➤ Find the Classified Ads — Help Wanted. Which job listed would you most like to have?

➤ Go through the whole newspaper, and look at the photographs. Which photo do you like the best? Can you think up a caption for it?

➤ Look at the editorial and letters to the editor pages. Discuss why these pages are included. Find other examples of fact and opinion in the paper.

➤ Play *Twenty Questions* with your family using names in the news.

Language:
Learning to Communicate

FOUR

Language: Learning to Communicate

The more a child is invited to practice and use language, the better he becomes at expressing himself. Being able to communicate with others is a skill he will need all his life.

A parent provides a child with his first role model for language. Every parent hears his own words and phrases, both desirable and undesirable, echoed by a youngster eager to learn to use language. It is therefore important that a parent take care to provide the best model possible for his child.

It is also important that a parent make an effort to correct mistakes, but subtly, without dulling the child's enthusiasm to learn. For instance, a parent who hears his child say, "The phone ringed when you were in the shower," can simply say, "Oh, the phone rang? Did you take a message for me?" Children hear more than we sometimes think they do. Indeed, they tend to have rather "big ears" at times!

The more time parents spend talking with their children, the better. The more words used, the larger the child's vocabulary becomes, and the more he will understand of what he hears and reads. Avoid baby talk, and don't be afraid to use "big words."

In addition to the role model presented by his parents, a child picks up words and phrases from both television and books. Most people tend to speak in phrases and run-on sentences. Therefore, reading books to a child provides an especially valuable model for communication, as stories are written in complete sentences and include a more varied vocabulary than that found in most everyday speech.

Listening, then, is obviously a vital part of communication and comprehension. How can a parent help his child learn to be a good listener? [See also, activities listed under "Auditory Discrimination" and "Auditory Memory" in chapter 2.]

★ A parent should take care to not speak too fast, and to be a good listener himself. Make eye contact with your child to let him know you are giving him your full attention.

★ Avoid repeating instructions needlessly and let your child know you are pleased when he shows he has listened carefully.

★ Ask questions about things he has read or heard, and encourage answers which show he has thought about the information and understands it.

Listening Activities

➤ Scramble a sentence orally and ask your child to re-arrange the words so that they make sense.

➤ See how many meanings your family can come up with for a particular word, such as: fair, plant, point, face, wash.

➤ Tape record a family conversation. Listen together as you play back the tape. Notice how often people speak in incomplete sentences. Simply becoming aware of how one speaks may encourage an attempt at better self-expression.

➤ Ask your child to listen for a particular word as you read a story to him. Each time he hears the word, he is to clap. Variations on this would be to have your child clap each time he hears a word which rhymes with a particular word, or every time he hears a noun.

➤ Find as many noise-making objects as possible and set them behind a screen of some sort, so that your child can't see them. Make a noise and ask your child to identify the object which made it. Objects might include: scissors, paper being torn, a rubber band being snapped, an egg beater, and so on.

➤ Play "Telephone." One person whispers a phrase into the ear of the person next to him, who in turn whispers what he heard into the ear of the person next to him, and so on until the last person has heard the message. He then repeats out loud what he heard. Chances are, the original message will have disappeared or been altered along the way.

The Power of the Written Word

Written communication is tied irrevocably to reading. Practical writing relays information and can be as simple as a grocery list or as involved as a report on the population of Alaska. It is writing with a purpose:

"Dear Jeff,

How did the Math test go? I have gone to the grocery store. Would you please set the table? Thanks!

Love,
Mom"

Creative writing, on the other hand, is meant to entertain:

"Fear is sitting in the creaking dentist's chair, seeing only the top of Dr. Rifkin's bald head as his trembling hand tries to zero in on a cavity."

This marvelous bit of descriptive writing, produced by a 12-year-old, is included in Harvey S. Wiener's book entitled, *Any Child Can Write: How To Improve Your Child's Writing Skills From Preschool Through High School.* In his book, Wiener stresses the importance of the parent's role in guiding his child's development of essential writing skills. The two main ingredients involved are ideas and correctness. "Nonsense correctly spelled and punctuated," says Wiener, "is still nonsense. Similarly, a set of brilliant ideas that follows none of the principles of correct writing falls apart."

The Beginning Writer

The child who is just beginning to write needs a different kind of attention than the older child who needs to improve upon his skills. More than anything else, the beginning writer needs encouragement. Make paper and pencils or markers easily accessible, and praise efforts to produce words, even if they are unrecognizable scribbles. Ask a child what he's written, and don't worry about what his paper looks like. The fact that the scribbles mean something to him, says that he grasps the concept of communication through writing. The more he is allowed to enjoy writing, the more eager he will be to learn to do it correctly, forming his letters and spelling his words carefully.

Once a child can form the letters of the alphabet easily, a parent can provide him with numerous opportunities to write.

Writing Activities

> Ask your child to add items to your grocery list for you. Offer to help with spelling. When you get to the store, let your child find the items he listed.

> Start a daily written exchange of ideas (news, compliments, greetings, or riddles) between your child and you. Leave a note on a chalkboard or piece of paper, leaving space for a written answer. Do the unexpected by including an occasional note with his lunch, or hiding one under his pillow or in the cookie jar.

> We all love to receive mail. Help your child make some special stationery for writing letters to relatives and friends. Suggest that he include a picture he's made or a recent photo showing him in a special activity. Try designing stationery on the computer at home or in school.

> Encourage your child to write any notes to his teacher concerning absences or the need to leave school early. He can sign them, and you can add your signature underneath his.

November 3, 1989

Dear Mrs. Iwon,

I have a doctor's appointment today in town. I need to be in the office at 2:00.

Thank you.

Sincerely,
Seth Gruba

Improving a Child's Writing Skills

O nce a child is capable of writing down thoughts, no matter how disorganized or incomplete they may be, he is ready for help. By this, I don't mean sitting down and teaching rules of grammar. Rather, I think a parent needs to make an effort to watch for opportunities to offer some informal guidance. If a child feels you are sincerely interested in hearing what he has written, he will share it with you and want your opinion. He won't continue to share, however, if you begin by pointing out all his mistakes. Tread softly when you deal with your child's creative writing. Writing is an art, and therefore subjective and connected to the ego.

Encourage your child to show you any stories or reports he writes for school or for his own enjoyment. Be sure to react to his efforts with positive words. Then ask him to read his work to you. This is the first step in learning to proofread, which is probably the most valuable writing skill you can help him acquire.

As he reads, you might want to look over his shoulder and watch to be sure that what he reads is what he indeed wrote, and not what he meant to write. Casually point out any words he omitted.

Did he remember to put ending punctuation in? If not, you can remind him, each time he pauses at the end of a sentence, to check for a period, question mark or exclamation point.

Make an effort to notice what he did well, and keep the majority of your comments positive. You don't need to correct every mistake on each and every paper. Just point out one or two things. If your child asks for more help, by all means give it!

Pointless exercises in writing, such as worksheets which ask a child to fill in a blank, are boring and generally nonproductive. Give a child a reason to write, challenge him to be creative, and he will usually be willing to comply.

Creative Writing Activities

➤ Encourage older children to write stories and make books for younger siblings. Suggest illustrations to accompany the stories. One idea would be a story about the younger sibling or the whole family.

➤ Ask your child to help you sort through and organize family photos. Encourage him to write captions for the pictures.

➤ Watch for things which a child can send for through the mail. Help him to write a letter requesting the material or item, and to address the envelope as well. *Free Things For Kids* (Meadowbrook Press) provides addresses and information on sending for a terrific variety of items, ranging from stamps to posters to informational booklets on topics such as pet care and solar energy.

➤ Seek your child's help in writing poems to include in homemade cards for family and friends. Once he gets the idea, he will probably try more on his own.

➤ Give your child a special notebook in which to keep a journal during a family vacation. He can write down the itinerary before you leave and keep track of places visited, mileage, special highlights and noteworthy events.

Encouraging Descriptive Writing

Parents can do a great deal to help their children create stories which are more satisfying for them to write as well as more fun for others to read. For instance, they can explain to their child that writing involves playing two different roles. First he must be a *creator* and allow ideas to flow onto his paper. It doesn't matter if they're silly, far-fetched, spelled perfectly or not, in complete sentences or not, because when he has exhausted his ideas, and turns to read what he has written, he will become his own *editor*. As editor, he needs to "fix" what he wrote, crossing out whatever he no longer wants included and inserting words he thinks are needed. His editing should include a review of spelling, punctuation and capitals. Finally, he should recopy his story neatly and read it once more to be sure the new version makes sense.

When helping their children with descriptive writing, parents should encourage the inclusion of as many sensory details as possible — words and phrases which describe colors, sounds, how something feels to the touch, what something smells or tastes like, details about the setting to help create a more complete picture. Questions like the ones below can help children develop more effective descriptions for their stories.

★ What time of year is it? Is there snow on the ground or rain streaming down the window panes? Are the tree branches bare or thick with leaves?

★ What time of day is it? Is it morning, afternoon, late at night? Are there lights on or is the room lit by sunlight? Are there shadows on the walls or on the character's face?

★ What colors stand out? What does the red in his shirt remind you of? As black as what? As white as a what?

★ What sounds are heard? Scratching, thumping, whispering, wailing sirens, a game show on the T.V., the dishwasher, a baby crying, or silence so thick your ears ring?

★ Are textures important? Does the character's hair remind you of smooth silk? Do his whiskers feel scratchy like sandpaper? Are her muscles hard like wood or soft like dough?

★ What smell is in the room? Perfume, a mustiness, the lemon scent from furniture polish, the smell of fried bacon? Does the character taste anything? What does it remind him of?

★ What words are spoken, if any? Are they shouted, whispered, mumbled, enunciated clearly?

Descriptive Writing Activities

➤ Have your child write a description of another member of the family. He might choose to do it from memory or through observation. Remind him of the types of details to consider as he writes.

➤ It is not uncommon for a child to want to write a story, but he may think he needs help coming up with an idea for it. If this happens, a parent can suggest writing a story which will explain how the kangaroo got its pocket, why the zebra has stripes, how the ocean got so salty, or why the grass is green. The more far-fetched the explanation, the better.

➤ Suggest to your child that he pretend he is an object such as a ping pong ball, a vacuum cleaner, or a door knob. He should create a name for himself, describe what he looks like, what he sounds like, where he lives, what his life is like.

➤ Get out old photographs and encourage your child to choose one of interest to him, study it, and write a few descriptive sentences which will make the photo come to life.

➤ Look together at the following examples and ask your child to make sentences from what is given. Make a point of looking for interesting sentence structure in books you read, and encourage your child to try incorporating them into his own writing.

★ **Because _____, we looked _____.** (For example: Because it was pouring, we looked like drowned rats when we got home. Because we were afraid, we looked for a place to hide. Because we were tired, we looked for a place to set up camp.)

★ **Laughing _____, the girl _____.**

★ **Running _____, the dog _____.**

★ **The man, _____, chased _____.**

★ **Swimming _____, the whale _____.**

★ **The old woman, _____, smiled _____.**

★ **Playing _____, the children _____.**

★ **Struggling _____, the little girl _____.**

★ **Sitting _____, the cat _____.**

★ **Afraid that _____, the boy _____.**

Writing a Report

C hildren in the upper elementary grades should be capable of producing a written assignment which follows the basic rules of punctuation, spelling, and grammar. The trick is to utilize them all effectively in one project.

Since most major assignments are expected to be completed over an extended period of time, a parent has the opportunity to help guide his child through the process of writing. It's extremely difficult for a teacher to meet regularly with individual students to work on the skills of writing and proofreading. There simply is not enough time. Instead, teachers take papers home, correct mistakes, write comments, and hope the student will look at and think about the corrections.

Many teachers have instituted writing workshops where students write, share their work with a partner, correct each other's work, as well as suggest and question. They then rewrite, confer again with the partner, and prepare a final draft for the teacher.

But the lesson a child must learn, is how to see and correct his mistakes on his own. Parents have a better opportunity than teachers to individually help children with this tremendous task.

Getting Started

When the assignment is first given, discuss the topic with your child. Encourage him to jot down ideas and words to be included. Take care not to give your child specific ideas; rather ask questions which will help him think of his own. Ask him to imagine all the questions someone might have about the topic. Help him get something down on paper, as getting started is the most difficult part of any writing assignment.

Taking Notes: Once a child understands what to look for, he needs to locate books, read and take notes. If you help your child learn to take notes, you will do him a great service. Good note-taking involves some skill, and the confidence that the student can reconstruct the information in his own words. Show him how to include only those words necessary to relay an idea and not copy word for word the information needed. You can practice by reading a passage from an encyclopedia together and writing down only the minimum of notes. Later show your child how he can turn his notes back into complete sentences using his own words.

Note-Taking Activities

➤ Taking notes involves writing down only key words and ideas. Below are some random passages of information which your child can use to practice note-taking. Remind your child that there are no "right" or "wrong" notes. Each person will have his own idea of which words are necessary to include.

Passages

★ Whether aquatic or not, all turtles lay their eggs on land, generally burying them or covering them with leaves.

★ Three kinds of weasel live in North America: the least weasel, the short-tailed weasel, and the long-tailed weasel. Birds and small rodents make up the main portion of a weasel's diet.

★ A giant kelp may grow at a rate of 2 feet a day. A kelp forest provides food and shelter for many kinds of marine animals such as otters, fish and octopuses.

★ On May 6, 1840, in Great Britain, the world's first adhesive postage stamp was issued. It was called the Penny Black and had an image of Queen Victoria on it.

★ Johnny Appleseed was an American folk hero who, in the early nineteenth century, spent years traveling through Pennsylvania, Ohio, Indiana and Illinois, planting apple seeds and encouraging the settlers to start orchards. His real name was John Chapman.

Notes
(Below are examples of the notes one might take on the passages.)

★ All turtles lay eggs on land — bury or cover w/ leaves

★ Three kinds of weasel in N. Am.: least, short-tailed and long-tailed. Eat mostly birds and small rodents

★ A giant kelp can grow 2 ft. a day; provides food and shelter for marine animals like otters, fish, octopus

★ May 6, 1840, in Great Britain, world's first adhesive postage stamp issued; called "Penny Black" — picture of Queen Victoria

★ Johnny Appleseed (real name John Chapman) in early 1800's traveled through Penn., Ohio, Indiana and Ill. planting apple trees; Am. folk hero

Try this kind of activity using newspaper articles, library books, magazine articles, and so on. You may even try taking notes as you listen to a T.V. news program. Taking notes is like any other skill. The more your child practices it, the easier it becomes.

Organizing Notes

Once your child has taken all his notes and written down the ideas he wants to include in his report, he needs to organize his thoughts. A teacher who wants a formal outline will usually lead students through this process. If an outline is not required, you can guide your child informally through this step, by asking him to decide which ideas belong together. He may want to number his notes. For example, in a report on pollution, he might mark all general, introductory comments as 1's, definitions of different kinds of pollution as 2's, problems created by pollution as 3's, solutions as 4's, and so on.

With his notes grouped appropriately, he simply needs to determine the order in which the different points in each group should be presented. He can do this as he makes a brief outline like the one below. If a formal outline is not required, keep it simple and don't worry about Roman numerals and letters.

POLLUTION
1. **Introduction**
   — **define pollution**
   — **why important issue**

2. Kinds of Pollution
   — Air
   — Water
3. Problems Created by Pollution
   — Health hazards
        — drinking water
        — air we breathe
   — Damage to ozone layer
        — effect on earth (temperature, water level)
        — increased danger to skin
4. Solutions
   — Control over industrial wastes — air and water
   — Improved education of consumers
   — Legislative

Once your child has an outline, he is ready to write. He can follow the order he has set up in his outline and refer to his notes for details.

The Rough Draft

Take time to explain that a rough draft is the first stage of writing, when a writer first puts down his ideas without worrying about being perfect. (Remind him of his two roles in writing — as creator, then editor.) Encourage your child to skip lines as he writes. The extra lines allow room for corrections, changes and additions he may need to make later as he edits. How messy this draft is and how many words are crossed out doesn't matter, as long as the paper is legible to him. No one else is going to read this version or judge its neatness. If he has trouble spelling a word, encourage him to spell it the best he can, and circle it so that he will remember to check on it later. Spelling should not be a major concern at this point.

Have your child read his finished rough draft aloud to you. Don't interrupt as he reads, and be sure your first response is a positive comment. ("You've got a lot of good information there!") Then, together go back and read one line at a time. Here you can ask questions to encourage more description or to complete an idea. Introduce the caret (^) for inserting additional words. Help your child find the mistakes he's made. (Does this make sense? How could you make it clearer? I see a place in the first line where a sentence should end. Can you find it? I see three spelling mistakes. Can you find them?) Encourage him to avoid too many "ands," instead writing shorter sentences, or using alternative joining words such as "since" or "because."

The Final Draft

Before begining the final draft, review points to remember in copying the paper over — margins, indenting, neatness, clear ending punctuation. After your child has copied his paper over, have him read it once again, looking to see that his spelling mistakes are corrected, that he hasn't inadvertently omitted a word, and that punctuation and capitals are where they should be. Have him read slowly, word by word, pointing to each word as he goes. Often we read what we expect to see, not what is actually there. There may still be a few mistakes, but that's O.K. Rome wasn't built in a day!

Remember to save your child's papers. Date them. Put them on the bulletin board for a while. Encourage him to share them with the rest of the family. Help him feel proud of the effort he's put into his work and to enjoy the satisfaction of a job well done.

Computers

Computers are not the "wave of the future" for our children. They are here now. The increase in the number of computers in the world has been dramatic in recent years. As their phenomenal capabilities continue to improve, they become increasingly indispensable. Our children can expect to use computers in their careers and their daily lives, making familiarity with them essential. Most elementary schools provide this introduction to computers. If your school is not actively working toward several computers in every classroom, as well as computer education for teachers and students, parents need to lobby for these things.

Dr. Faith Clark, of the Human Development Clinic, explains the advantages of a computer learning program over a human tutor: a computer "has endless time, emotional neutrality, patience, and the ability to keep giving positive reinforcement in the face of a seemingly endless series of wrong answers." Computers not only free teachers for one-to-one time with their students, but sometimes can be more efficient in teaching.

Writing with a Computer

Many students nowadays do most of their writing assignments on the computer. It is not unusual for a fifth or sixth grader to feel completely comfortable working from the rough draft to the final draft at the keyboard.

The interesting thing about this is that students who work at a computer tend to put at least as much time into their work as those who write reports longhand. In fact, computer-written reports tend to be more fully developed because the rewrite process goes more smoothly.

There are some very basic word processing programs which have been developed for use by students. Two that come to mind are *First Choice* and *Q and A*, although there are many others. Be sure that the program is easy enough for the student to use; after all, the assignment should be the focal point of the student's attention. (You might want to see what kind of word processing program is used by the school in the classrooms before purchasing one.)

Two features of a good word processing program for children are the "spell-check" and the thesaurus. Spell-check programs actually help poor spellers learn to spell. When asked to check a document's spelling, the computer scans every word, stopping when it picks up one it does not recognize, such as "atenion." The computer will then ask the student to consider five possible choices for the correct spelling: intention, attention, addition, tension, or "other." The student must choose one or spell the word he really meant.

The thesaurus is an excellent tool for helping the writer expand vocabulary and begin to see the nuances in language. Again, the thesaurus works by giving the student choices. At first, you might have to say, "Isn't there another word to use instead of 'fast'?" By asking for a clarification, and indirectly sending the writer to the thesaurus, you encourage the use of precise language.

Many students who have difficulty with incomplete sentences can both hear and see them more clearly on a computer print-out than on a hand-written paper. Somehow the type-written page forces us to see what we have actually written, rather than what we think we have written. Spelling errors also tend to be more visible.

Because spelling and grammatical errors are so much easier to correct on a computer, it is not unreasonable to expect a somewhat higher degree of accuracy in final drafts. Also, students should be encouraged to set margins, titles, name, and date with care. There is no acceptable excuse for anything but a neat, well-spaced paper when it is computer printed.

Computers and Software

If you already own a personal computer, you have undoubtedly found it to be a worthwhile purchase for the whole family. The most difficult question you face is, "Which software should I buy?"Generally speaking, you want to look for software which is interactive, requiring your child to respond with more than the press of a single button.Although a few software programs are mentioned by name in this book, I won't attempt to offer a lengthy list of specific titles for the simple reason that by the time this book is published, there will be newer and possibly better programs on the market. Look for programs which actively involve your child and stimulate his brain, are fun and easy to use. Ask to try out any software before you buy it.

If you don't own a computer but are considering a purchase, check to see what kinds are used in your school system. A great deal of frustration can be eliminated if you purchase a system your child is already familiar with. The same is true of software.

Check into the possibility of joining a local computer club. A club can provide useful contacts and information, including sources of "public-domain" software which cost far less than that of commercial programs, usually $5.00 or less per disk. As with commercial programs, there are good and bad among the public-domain software. It is worth the effort to do a little research before purchasing either type for your child's or your own use.

Most parents of upper elementary and older children are probably aware of the increasing number of computerized games being produced. There are a few educational computer games worth looking into, but many of the other games have few, if any redeeming qualities. While they are extremely popular, these games, like television, promote antisocial behavior. It may be unrealistic to try and eliminate these games completely from your child's life, but you can and should set limits, just as you do with television.

Spelling

"Beware of heard, a dreadful word
That looks like beard and sounds like bird."

The above simply reminds one of how fickle the English language is, with all its inconsistencies. There are different spellings for the same sound, and different sounds for the same letter combinations! No wonder children (and adults!) often have difficulty with spelling!

Much has been written about poor spellers: Is there such a thing? Are they just lazy? Does poor spelling indicate a learning disability? Without getting into the scientific data, it is fair to say that some very bright students, with very helpful parents and very creative teachers have not been able to spell. An excellent, brief article on spelling, "Can't Spell? Yur Not Dumm," by Melinda Beck, can be found in the June 6, 1988 issue of *Newsweek*. It's definitely worth reading if spelling is an issue in your household.

We've all seen students who studiously learn their weekly spelling lists, achieve 100 percent on their quizzes, and two weeks later misspell half the words. These same students are often very creative, avid readers and intellectually curious. In fact, oftentimes poor spellers are at the top of their class.

For these students, parents should proceed with the exercises that follow, especially the use of mnemonic devices. In addition, parents and teachers may want to help chronic misspellers learn to use aides such as computer spell-check programs. The goal is for the poor speller to learn how to avoid having poor spelling detract from his written expression.

Ultimately, whether one is a "naturally" good speller or must rely on a dictionary or a computer's spell-check for help doesn't matter. What is important for a child to understand is that materials written for others to read should not include misspelled words.

There are many ways in which a parent can help his child learn to spell. Perhaps the best enhancement to spelling skills is reading; for many children the more they read, the better they spell. Below are some things to keep in mind, as well as game ideas for both primary and upper elementary grade children.

Keep in mind:

★ For many, spelling is a visual skill. A word either "looks right," or it doesn't. Encourage the use of visual cues along with the basic rules of phonics.

★ Children spell what they hear. It is therefore important that parents pronounce words carefully. If they say "breffast" for "breakfast," their children will most likely spell the word incorrectly.

★ If you want to help your child prepare for weekly spelling tests, encourage him to bring home his list of words early in the week, so that you can work with him on 5 words each night, rather than all 20 on the night before the test.

★ You can help your child by pointing out similarities among words involving root words and origins. It helps a child to learn to recognize the relationship (in spelling and meaning) between words such as divide, division, indivisible.

★ While some children learn to spell by writing or tracing a word a few times or perhaps having someone quiz them orally, others need to manipulate letters in order to imprint the different combinations on their brains. Letter cards or tiles are helpful for these children. Other children learn to spell most easily if they combine spelling aloud with a rhythmic movement, be it tapping a pencil on the table, writing in the air or marching in place. Use what you know about your child's learning style to determine how he will learn to spell most easily.

★ Children tend to be fairly consistent in their spelling errors. Try to identify any errors your child makes repeatedly, look for a pattern, and help him correct the problem.

★ Mnemonic devices can help a child remember how to spell a word. An example is: "He is a fri*end* to the *end*," to remind you that friend is spelled with "ie" rather than "ei."

Encourage your child to create mnemonic devices to help him with "problem words." It is best for each person to think up his own word associations. The weirder an association is, the better it will be remembered. Other examples would be: "Ma and *pa* are in se*pa*rate cars" to remember to use "a" and not "e" in the middle syllable of the word; "Never bel*ie*ve a *lie*" to remind you to use "ie" and not "ei."

★ It helps to be aware of some of the words most commonly misspelled by students. Below are 50 such words to pay special attention to:

across	**amount**	**believe**
all right	**argument**	**breathe**
among	**beautiful**	**chief**

coming	opportunity	recommend
embarrass	parallel	rhythm
experience	particular	safety
height	personal	sense
heroes	personnel	separate
interest	possible	similar
led	practical	succeed
lose	preferred	surprise
necessary	prepare	than
ninety	principal	then
occur	principle	unnecessary
occurred	privilege	woman
opinion		

★ It is important to take some time to discuss those words which sound alike but are spelled differently and mean different things (homonyms). Errors are commonly made misusing:

**to, two, too
their, there, they're
its, it's**

Spelling Games for the Primary Grade Child

➤ "I am in see, sing and say. What sound am I?"
"I am in look, but not in took. I am __." And so on.

➤ **Endless Chain:** The first player starts by spelling any word he wants to spell. The next player spells a word that begins with the last letter of the word spelled by the first player, and so on. This can also be done by one child, perhaps writing his name, and then continuing the chain with the names of children in his class. ("John — Nancy — Yolanda — Allen.")

➤ Place a set of alphabet cards or tiles, face down, on a table. Decide on a category (such as animals, birds, food, sports), and as each player picks up a card, he must name or write a word beginning with that letter and belonging to the category decided upon.

➤ Scramble the letters of a word for your child to rewrite correctly, after you have given him a short definition or clue.

➤ Write a word like "hat."Have your child make all the words he can by changing just the first letter, (cat, bat, fat, and so on) or by changing the vowel (hot, hit, hut).

Spelling Games For Upper Elementary Child

➤ You can adapt most of the games described above for older children.

➤ Memory Game: Say 3 words. Your child listens and writes them down. Increase the number of words.

➤ Ghost: One person starts with a letter that is also a word (as "a" or "I"). The next person adds another letter to make still another word as "in." The third child might spell "tin," and the fourth, "into." The letters may be rearranged, but each previous letter must be included and just one new letter added. The child who cannot make a new word in this way is a ghost. The object is not to become a ghost!

➤ Play "Hangman." Player 1 thinks of a word and draws on a piece of paper the same number of spaces as there are letters in his word. He also draws a hangman's tree:

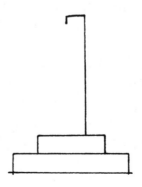

Player 2, who is trying to guess Player 1's word, should write on his own piece of paper, the letters of the alphabet. He then plays by guessing one letter at a time. If the letter is in the word, the first player writes it in the correct space. If the letter is not in the word, Player 1 draws one part of a body on the hangman's tree (Sounds morbid, doesn't it?), and Player 2 crosses the letter off his alphabet. The goal is for Player 2 to guess the word before he gets hung. (It's up to the players to decide how many body parts are required to hang someone.)

➤ A number of commercially produced games including *Boggle, Spill & Spell, Probe* and *Scrabble* have been created to encourage spelling.

"Writing quotations isn't so bad!" she admitted.

While writing quotations poses a great problem for many children, it needn't be that tricky. It is, however, an area in which most children need a little extra help.

There are three basic forms of quotation. The easiest way to describe them is to write the same sentence in the three different ways:

Form 1: John said, "Writing quotations is really quite simple."
Form 2: "Writing quotations is really quite simple," said John.
Form 3: "Writing quotations," said John, "is really quite simple."
Now let's look more closely at the correct punctuation.

Form 1: This is the simplest form. First, enclose the spoken words in quotation marks. Then place a comma between the first unspoken words and the quotation, and remember to use the proper punctuation and end quotation marks. Be sure to begin the quotation with a capital.
Sue asked, "Where are you going?"
Michael said, "I am going to the store."

The ending punctuation of the quotation can be tricky. *The period, question mark or exclamation point always belongs inside (before) the final quotation marks.* Remember, too, that the final punctuation of the quotation serves as the final punctuation for the sentence in Form 1.

You may find it helpful to give your child some sentences to practice on:

1. Dad asked who would like to go with me
2. Peter said I thought your car was blue

Have your child think up a few more sentences which follow this pattern.

Form 2: In this form, there are three situations to consider:

1. In a simple statement, you put a comma after the words spoken and a period at the end of the sentence.

"I am going to the store," said James.

2. If the speaker is asking a question, *the question mark follows the question — it does NOT come at the end of the sentence* — and a period is placed at the end.

"What are you doing?" asked Mark.

3. If the speaker shouts something excitedly, the quotation is followed by an exclamation point, and the sentence by a period.

"Watch out!" cried Meg.

The tricky part seems to be the fact that the stronger, expressive punctuation in these last two examples comes after the words *spoken* and *not* at the end of the sentence. But, if you think about it, that makes sense; the excitement is in the actual quotation, where it belongs.

Practice sentences:

1. I read a good book last week said Mark
2. Would you like to play football asked Loren

Form 3: In this form of quotation, the words spoken are split into two parts. You simply want to remember to place a comma after the first part of the quotation and again after the words not spoken. The appropriate punctuation comes at the end of the quotation. Do not capitalize the beginning of the second part of the quotation.

"I like both chocolate," said Mike, "and vanilla."

Practice sentences:
1. I'd like to go said Fred but I can't
2. How cried Mrs. Smith did you get so dirty

Encourage your child to use quotations when he writes stories. They add life to the characters. Help him come up with alternatives to "said." For instance, he might consider the following if they seem appropriate: remarked, questioned, yelled, replied, cried, shouted, answered.

Creative Language Activities

(See page 130 for answers.)

➤ Invite your child to write a story, and hand him a camera and a roll of film. Encourage him to utilize different and interesting local people and places in his story and photos.While the film is at the processor's, your child can make a book and copy his story onto the pages, leaving spaces for the photos. A variation on this for older children is to have them script a "guided tour" or story, and then using a camcorder, produce a video with narration.

➤ A treasure hunt is a great activity which utilizes a number of skills of communication — reading clues, discussing possible meanings, looking for puns and language nuances. I can almost guarantee that if a parent is willing to do a little planning beforehand, he can create an activity which children will love. Chances are that after participating in one or two treasure hunts, the children will plan their own, in which case the activity will also include the skill of writing.

The nice thing about treasure hunts is that they can be created for any age child. Picture clues work well for preschoolers, beginning readers can use clues which consist of only a word or two, while older children are most challenged by subtle clues, secret codes, poems with special meaning, and so on.

Sample Clues:

★ Bugs Bunny eats me. *(to lead to the carrots in the refrigerator)*

★ I tell you what time it is. *(a clock)*

★ With me, you can talk to your friends even when you can't see them. *(a telephone)*

★ Set up a coded message to spell out a clue: *(1=A, 2=B...)*
    9 11 5 5 16 20 8 9 14 7 19 3 15 12 4
    ("I keep things cold" to lead to the refrigerator.)

★ I produce oxygen and have chlorophyll. *(a plant)*

★ I swallowed my vitamin _____ + the opposite of high *(to lead the child to look under his pillow)*

★ Make a picture clue:

(To grow, I need sun, water, carbon dioxide. — a plant!)

★ If you have a collection of record albums, choose the title of a song to suggest which album cover holds the next clue.

★ Ask questions which will require looking in the dictionary or encyclopedia.
    What is the capital of Sweden?
    Who was the 27th president of the U.S.?
    What is the scientific name for salt?

★ Familiar neighbors' telephone numbers could have your children running to several houses to look under the appropriate telephones for clues.

> **Plays and skits:** Most children love to act. They do it from the time they are prescshoolers, pretending to be princesses, cops and robbers, moms and dads, even animals. Parents need to encourage creativity — acting is an easy way to do it. Offer old clothes for costumes, help with makeup and props, provide old sheets and clothesline for curtains, and find materials which will create needed sound effects.

A child who tends to be inhibited may need some help getting started on a play. You might suggest a skit based upon a favorite fairy tale or story. Look for plays in children's reading texts or magazines. Search the library for books of plays for children. And help your child create and write original plays — comedies, musicals, mysteries, whatever he most wants to try!

If your child and friends get serious, and work on their play over an extended period of time, they may want to make a stage, scenery, and programs. Have them make posters and invite family and neighbors to come to see it! Then find a seat in the audience and enjoy!

Playing With Words!

> **Word bridges:** Ask your child for a word. Write it vertically, forward and backward as in the example below:

H	E
O	S
R	R
S	O
E	H

The goal is to create words to fill in the gaps. For instance, one might make HOME or HIDE using the first pair of letters. Two or more people might compete by each writing the words on their own papers and seeing who can finish first. Older children might want to put a time limit on the game and give a point for each letter added between the two given letters.

> **Who am I?** This is an old favorite where each person has the name of a famous person pinned to his back.

His job is to determine "who he is," by asking the other people questions. The one rule is that the questions can only be answered "yes" or "no." (Questions would include: Am I alive? Am I a man? Am I a movie star? and so on.)

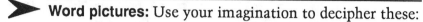

Word pictures: Use your imagination to decipher these:

a. <u>wear</u>
   long

b. i R i I i G i H i T i

c. GEGS
   GGES
   EGGS

d. $\boxed{\text{SAND}}$

e. BAN   ANA

f. <u>stand</u>
   I

g. ⬭ROSEY⬭

h. ◻ (illustration of a large numeral "1" with a small circle)

i. <u>man</u>
   board

j. YOUJUSTME

k. $\boxed{\text{WAGON}}$

l. NEFRIENDED

m. D E
   A L

Hint: The answer to (a) is "long underwear." Perhaps the best part of puzzles like this is that once you do a few of them, you almost automatically start creating your own. I have no doubt that you and your child will come up with more.

Analogies: Below are some analogies to help your child look for ways in which things are related.

Example: HOT is to COLD as UP is to
            over / under /⬭down⬭/ high
a. ANCHOR is to BOAT as BRAKE is to
   car/ stop / wheel / crash

b. HALLOWEEN is to OCTOBER as CHRISTMAS is
to Santa Claus / December / snow / Sunday

c. PICKLES are to JAR as GRAIN is to
field / water / silo / satin

d. YEAR is to AUGUST as WEEK is to
Friday / fortnight / month / century

e. STONE is to QUARRY as LUMBER is to
wood / mine / leaves / forest

f. WOOD is to DECAY as IRON is to
dampness / rust / steel / ore

g. SHOWER is to CLOUDBURST as WIND is to
rain / sunshine / climate / cyclone

h. DOG is to CANINE as CAT is to
bovine / masculine / feline / tiger

i. MAN is to OMNIVOROUS as LION is to
kingly / animal / carnivorous / omnipotent

j. CAR is to BUMPER as KNIGHT is to
steel / man / armor / charger

➤ **Add a little something:** By inserting the same letter 13
times in the appropriate places, this jumble of letters
will be transformed into a sentence of some sense:

**V R Y V N I N G R N S T A R N D I G H T N C N T S
A S I L Y**

➤ **How Y's are you?** Add a "Y" to each word below, and
rearrange the letters to form a new word. (For example:
Add a "Y" to THOU and you get YOUTH.)

a. GRIND b. BEAM c. SEAT d. PALER e. ORAL

➤ **Palindromes:** For fun, see how many palindromes you
and your child can come up with. Palindromes are
words which are spelled the same from left to right and
from right to left. (For example: "noon" or "pup.")

➤ **Little words:** (We've all played this one!) Ask your child
to choose a nice long word and then see how many
little words each of you can make from the letters in
the long word. Set a time limit on the game to keep it
from dragging.

➤ **Letter ladders:** Try to climb down the ladder, changing
the word on the top rung to the word on the bottom

rung, by altering one letter on each step. (Each step must be a word.)

Example: Go from "man" to "boy" in 4 steps:

MAN
BAN
BAY
BOY

a. HIM

    _____

   HER

b. FIRE

    _____

    _____

    _____

   COLD

➤ **Hink pinks:** Ask your child to figure these puzzles out. The trick is that the answers must be made of 2 words that rhyme, each one syllable long.

a. What is a hink pink for an angry father?
b. What is a hink pink for a fat fish?
c. What is a hink pink for a tiny sphere?
d. What is a hink pink for an angry employer?
e. What is a hink pink for an obese feline?

    Once your child gets the hang of these, encourage him to create his own. He might also want to create "Hinky Pinkies" which are like Hink Pinks, but the answers have two syllables instead of one.

➤ **Dictionary:** One player chooses from the dictionary, a word he thinks no one will be familiar with (the stranger the better!). After telling the other players what the word is, he copies down the definition on a piece of paper. The other players make up their own definitions for the word and write them down. When everyone is finished, the one who chose the word mixes up all the definitions and reads them aloud. The others then try to guess the true definition of the word.

➤ **Word squares:** Each player draws a square on a piece of paper and divides it into 16 smaller squares — 4 across, 4 down. Players agree on a 4-letter word and each writes it in the squares across the top and down the left side of his square. The object of the game is to finish the square by filling letters into the other boxes to make words which are the same horizontally and vertically. The first player to finish his square wins.

Example:

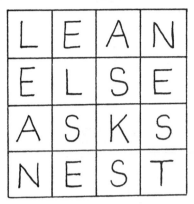

Categories: Players choose 4 or 5 categories and list them down the left side of their papers. Then they decide on a 5-letter word to be written across the page, above and to the right of the list of categories. Draw lines to make a chart like the one below. The object is to fill in the boxes, by finding for each category, a word that begins with the letter at the top of the column. At the end of a specific period of time (agreed upon earlier), exchange papers and score together. If a word is correct, the player receives as many points as there are other players who did not have that word on their papers, so try to be correct and unusual in your answers.

Example:

	S	T	A	M	P
COUNTRY	Spain	Tibet	Austria	Monaco	Peru
FOOD	sausage	tostado	artichoke	mayonnaise	pizza
ANIMAL	scorpion	tiger	antelope	mountain lion	porcupine
MUSICAL INSTRUMENT	snare drum	trombone	autoharp	maraca	piccolo

Knock knocks and puns: A difficult concept for some children to grasp is the idea that a word or phrase can have more than one meaning. Knock Knock jokes encourage a child to see how a word can "change" into another in a silly way. Libraries usually have a number of Knock Knock books. Encourage your child to learn some jokes and ask family and friends to "play." (Example: Knock knock. — Who's there? — Eileen. — Eileen who? — Eileen'd on the fence too hard and it broke!)

Answers to Puzzles

Word Pictures:
a. long underwear
b. right between the eyes
c. scrambled eggs
d. sand box
e. banana split
f. I understand
g. ring around the rosey
h. a hole in one
i. man overboard
j. just between you and me
k. covered wagon
l. friend in need
m. a square deal

Analogies:
a. car
b. December
c. silo
d. Friday
e. forest
f. rust
g. cyclone
h. feline
i. carnivorous
j. armor

Add A Little Something:
Every evening Earnest earned eighteen cents easily.

How Y's Are You?
a. drying b. maybe c. yeast d. player (or pearly) e. royal

Letter Ladders:
a. Him
  Hem
  Her

b. Fire
  Fore
  Core
  Cord

Hink Pinks:
a. mad dad
b. stout trout
c. small ball
d. cross boss
e. fat cat

Math Can Be Fun!

F I V E

Math Can Be Fun!

Math is all around us. So are the opportunities to make math come alive for our children. This chapter offers some explanations of how you can work with your child to be sure he develops a comfortable relationship with numbers. This involves the child not only acquiring basic math skills, but even more importantly, understanding how to use them.

Although girls start off doing at least as well as boys in math, their performance starts to lag in early adolescence. By high school, boys consistently outscore girls on math achievement tests, and the enrollment of boys in advanced math classes far surpasses that of girls. The reason for this great difference in math achievement has been the topic of a considerable amount of study and controversy.

Researcher Camille Benbow is well known for her study of precocious math students who, before the age of 13, scored 700 or higher on the math section of the S.A.T.'s. Benbow found that boys are 12 times more likely than girls to be in this group. She also found a strong tendency to be left-handed, myopic and allergic. Benbow believes that biological as well as environmental factors are responsible. This notion has been criticized by some and supported by others.

The late Norman Geschwind, a neurologist at Harvard Medical School, as well as others, suggested that the physical characteristics discovered by Benbow's study are related to the fetus's exposure to high levels of testosterone in the womb. It is believed that testosterone inhibits the development of the left hemisphere. According to Geschwind, this would cause the right hemisphere in boys to compensate by developing more rapidly, possibly creating greater spatial visualization and mathematical reasoning abilities in the developing male child.

Other researchers feel that differences in math aptitude are due instead to environmental and social influences placed on children in our society. Certainly, until recent years, the need for girls to learn advanced math was questioned by many, because it wasn't expected that they would seek jobs requiring these skills. Consequently, parents didn't encourage girls as much as they did boys in the area of math skills. Unfortunately, many parents still fail to envision their daughters in math-related occupations and therefore don't encourage the development of math skills.

At home, boys are generally provided with many more construction toys to play with than are girls. As a result, boys tend to be more comfortable with geometry and spatial concepts than girls.

The "boys will be boys" attitude is also offered as a reason for the greater interest on the part of boys in the area of math. Teachers seem to allow boys to interrupt and ask questions more than they do girls, who are expected to be quiet and well-mannered. As a result, in many classrooms boys get more help than girls do, and feel freer to speak up and risk an incorrect answer. Boys also tend to be more aggressive in pursuing math work on the classroom computer.

As there is no agreement on the issue of sexual differences as they relate to math aptitude, parents should proceed on the belief that they can influence children's attitudes toward math. They can help children feel comfortable using numbers and encourage them to see math as an enjoyable means of challenging one's brain. Here are some ways to make math attractive to both boys and girls:

★ Let them know that math is as important as reading.

★ Encourage them to play with blocks, construction sets, and puzzles, thereby helping them to discover how things are put together and come apart and how they exist spatially.

★ Encourage computer use with math-related software.

★ Introduce them to men and women who like and excel in math-related fields; e.g. doctors, accountants, scientists, teachers.

★ Play lots of math games, solve lots of puzzles, have fun with math together.

★ Investigate the school's attitude toward math. Is math as high a priority as reading? Is the classroom teacher enthusiastic about math? Does she accomodate different learning styles? Does she encourage and challenge the girls as much as she does the boys?

Learning Math

T he nice thing about math is that unlike reading, which involves dealing with symbols (letters) which represent other symbols (words), math involves dealing with symbols which can be related to things which are tangible and real. The more young children "play" with numbers and number concepts using concrete materials, the easier it is for them to deal with the written, symbolic form of math later on.

Therefore, it is essential that children be provided with lots of materials and encouraged to manipulate, put in order, count, contrast, construct, reorganize — in short, experience the concepts of math. Parents need to keep in mind that this period of discovery takes time. Each child must be allowed to work at his own speed and without pressure to move on until he is comfortable with the basics. Most children are not able to use numbers with any real sense of confidence until they are between 6 1/2 and 8 years old. Until they reach this level of "operational facility," written assignments — which involve the use of symbols — are apt to create a great deal of confusion for children.

Adults often assume that a child who can count understands the concept of numbers and is ready to deal in symbols. We need to be reminded of the ambiguities a child must deal with. For instance, '=' does not always mean 'is equal to,' because 1 does not always equal 1 (1 foot does not equal 1 mile). Obvious to us, but not so simple to a child who is suddenly having to deal with different 1's!

Many children in first grade can handle simple addition, subtraction, multiplication, and division, in concrete form. Yet, many are not able to perform these same operations in writing until well into the second grade. Dealing with math symbols is still hard for most children even into third grade.

By the time a child reaches the intermediate grades, if he has developed a comfortable relationship with the basics of math, he is able to grasp the idea that addition and subtraction nullify each other, as do multiplication and division. He understands that multiplication is based on addition, and he is intrigued with the idea of multiplying by alternative methods. This is the age when the child is ready to be challenged by math and should be invited to try the brain teaser type of activities provided in the next chapter. He needs to see that math can be fun!

A parent who plays math games with his child, who works with him on solving puzzles, and shares with him a genuine enjoyment of the challenges math offers, increases the liklihood that his child will enjoy math and pursue it in high school and beyond.

When a Child Is Having Trouble

A child should not be pushed into dealing with math symbols or complex operations before he has a firm grasp on basic number concepts. Parents need to be able to determine when a child simply needs more time in order to grasp a concept, and when he has a real problem which requires their help.

When they see their child making mistakes, the first question they should ask is, "Does the problem lie in the child's failure to understand a particular math concept, or is there a physical cause?" A child who writes a "3" backwards but correctly identifies it as a three and shows a grasp of the concept of "threeness," does not have a math problem. He has a visual perception problem. Usually, this type of reversal corrects itself in time, and should not cause great concern.

A child who has trouble adding large numbers may know his facts and the process to follow, but has a hard time lining up his answers. This child also has a visual perception problem. He may benefit from using graph paper or holding his paper so that the lines run vertically.

If a parent suspects that his child's problem involves an inadequate grasp of math, the "treatment" is almost always the same: return to the concrete. Provide hands-on, manipulative materials to play and experiment with until the child can literally see what you are talking about. Bring out piles of Popsicle sticks, toothpicks, M&M's or buttons. Help group them with elastic bands or within a circle of yarn. Touch objects while counting aloud. Play the games in this chapter over and over, until "the light comes on" and the child is ready to move on.

It is not uncommon for children to suddenly have difficulty in math when story problems are introduced, usually in third grade. If this combination of words with numbers proves confusing to your child, simply take him back to the concrete. Have him "act out" the problems, and handle objects until he learns which operations are meant by which words. (For instance, "how many in all" means you have to add, and "how many are left" means to subtract, and so on.) As you work on story problems together, it might be helpful to write down the commonly used phrases and the operation indicated by each. Let your child refer to the list as long as he needs to.

Recognizing the Numbers Activities

While many children can count from memory when they are quite young, it takes a while for them to understand the one-to-one correspondence between a number and a specific quantity. It takes even longer to be able to match the written number with its name. There are numerous games which can help a child learn to recognize numbers and their values.

➤ Divide a piece of paper or cardboard into 8 squares (two rows of four), and have your child choose a number (from 1 to 9) for each square. After writing the numbers in the squares, hand your child a coin. Have him throw it onto the paper as many times as necessary until it lands on a square. He may then take the matching number of paper clips (or poker chips, buttons, whatever) from the "Bank." Now it is your turn. After you have each taken a second turn, stop and count aloud the number of paper clips you each have accumulated. The one with the most clips is the winner. When your child is ready for higher numbers, throw 3 or 4 times before stopping to count.

➤ Variations on "Bingo" games can help with number recognition. Start by making up some Bingo "boards" with numbers 0 through 9. Next make up the individual cards with numbers which match in some way. For instance, each individual card might show a certain number of objects, requiring the child to count the objects and decide if he has the corresponding number on his board. Another game would involve matching the word "four" on a card with the number "4" on the board, and so on.

2	5	7
4	9	3
1	8	6

➤ On your driveway, carport or other washable cement-type surface, draw a huge number in chalk. (Stick with the same number until your child recognizes it with ease.) Ask your child to walk slowly over it, following with his feet the same movement one's hand makes when drawing the number.

➤ Decorate your house (or kitchen or child's room) with a number of the week. Use the numeral, the number written out, the number illustrated, the number in coins, even the number in Roman numerals. Then, use the number frequently. For example, bake 5 monster cookies, buy 5 pieces of penny candy, buy 5 new guppies for a fish bowl, exchange 5 pennies for a nickel, and so on.

Math Facts

Math facts have long been a problem for many children and thus, for their teachers and parents, too. It is painful to watch children in the sixth grade struggling to count on their fingers, yet it happens all the time.

If your child is in the first or second grade, you can begin working on the basic facts of addition and subtraction. If he is in the third grade, you might want to check with his teacher to see if the class is working on multiplication facts yet. From the fourth grade on, it is extremely important to deal with multiplication and division facts as well as reinforcing addition and subtraction facts.

In learning math facts, there is actually no teaching involved. (This is assuming that the child understands the basic concepts involved, but simply hasn't committed the facts to memory yet.) It is really the child's responsibility to memorize, but a parent can help by playing games at home and by stressing the importance of learning these facts. The sooner the child can respond quickly and automatically, the easier all further computation will be.

Begin with addition facts no matter what grade your child is in, checking to be sure there are no lingering troublesome facts. By the sixth grade especially, all facts should be answered without hesitation.

Some children like using flash cards. Triangular flash cards, in particular, can help a child become familiar with the three numbers involved in each math fact. Blank index cards cut diagonally in half work fine. Each triangle presents an entire "family of facts." The one below shows the relationship between the numbers 4, 5 and 9. Triangular flash cards can also be used when first presenting multiplication and division facts.

This one card shows:

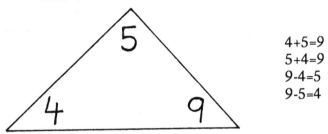

4+5=9
5+4=9
9-4=5
9-5=4

When you hold up each card, ask your child to say all four facts.

When using regular rectangular flash cards, where the problem is written on the front and the answer on the back, it is often helpful to have the child read the whole problem aloud and then give the answer. This adds the dimension of hearing, which is the way some children learn best. Try to keep the drill moving as quickly as possible.

Once your child has developed a little more confidence in his ability to answer correctly, let him race against the clock. See how many facts he correctly answers in one minute. Try again and see if he can beat his own record.

When working on addition facts, point out that numbers can be added in any order. (This is called the Commutative Property.) In other words, 3+2=2+3. You really don't have to learn two facts, just one combination of two numbers!

Keep in mind that some children need to count on their fingers longer than others. It would slow their progress if they were forced to not use their fingers when needed, and at the same time increase their anxiety about not being "smart enough." In this case, play more games to practice and reinforce the facts. Eventually fingers won't be needed.

The nice thing about subtraction facts is that your child has already dealt with the same numbers in addition, only in reverse. Explain the relationship between numbers in an addition fact and its reverse, the subtraction facts. (Triangular flash cards show this relationship well.)

When dealing with multiplication (or division) facts, it is usually easiest to deal with one "number" at a time. For instance, start with the 5's, as they are the easiest. When your child has mastered the 5's, work on the 10's and then the 2's. Go on to the 3's and 4's, and leave the 7's, 8's and 9's for last as they are the most difficult. By the time your child reaches these harder sets of facts, he will already actually know most of them, but in reverse. (He will know 9 X 5, because he learned 5 X 9 way back in the beginning.) Check to see that your child can count by 5's (or 10's or 2's, etc.) before you start working on the facts involved.

Help your child see that multiplication is really a form of addition. If he has trouble figuring out a particular fact, show him how he can go to what he knows and add or subtract to get the answer he needs. For instance, if he can't remember 8 X 6, but knows that 8 X 5 equals 40, he should go to what he knows and add another 8 (40+8=48).

Hints for Working on 9's:

★ The first number in the answer is always one less than the number you are multiplying 9 by. Also, the two numbers of the answer always add up to 9! For example:

9 x 6 = 54   **The "5" in the answer is one less than the "6" you multiplied by, and 5 + 4 equals 9.**

★ You might want to show your child the following "trick" which can help when he gets stuck on a "9" fact. Have him hold both his hands out in front of him, thumbs close to each other, fingers straight and spread comfortably. Tell him that to find the answer to 9 x 3,

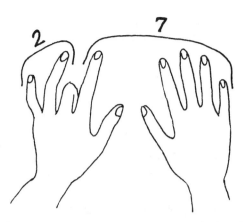

he simply bends down his 3rd finger and looks at the remaining fingers. In this case, there are two up, then the one bent down, and seven more up. Using the "up" fingers, he knows the answer is 2, then 7, or 27. Give him more facts to try this way. He can use the technique which simply aims to help him while he is learning. Eventually he won't need to use it.

★ When working on division, present the idea of number families again, if you didn't already with multiplication facts. Show your child that division is simply multiplication in reverse, and the same three numbers are involved in each of the four facts in the family. If your child is having trouble visualizing what division means, get out a pile of M&M's or buttons or straws, and let him manipulate them to find the answers. For instance, to solve 15÷3= __, have him take 15 buttons and divide them into 3 equal piles. How many buttons are in each pile?

Math Games

➤ Bingo-type games can easily be made with numbers on a board and addition problems on the individual cards.

➤ Draw a "ladder" on a piece of posterboard or paper. Write the numbers from 0 through 9 in the spaces between the rungs, in random order. Ask your child to roll a die. In order to climb the ladder, he must correctly add the number rolled to the numbers leading to the top. If he incorrectly answers a problem, he falls off the ladder! THUD! Now it's your turn. Tell your child that as you climb the ladder, answering the problems, you will intentionally make a mistake. His job is to catch the mistake, in which case you tumble to the ground. The object is simply to see how many times you can make it to the top of the ladder without falling.

➤ Write a number in the bottom of each egg carton section, making some of them "minus." Give your child and yourself each the same number of a different small object, such as pennies or buttons or pebbles. Take turns tossing the objects into the egg carton. When all the objects have been tossed, each person totals up his own points.

➤ "Concentration" can be adapted to learning any set of math facts. To play, you will need to make pairs of cards. In each pair, one card should have a math fact problem (7-3) and the other card, the answer (4). Make as many pairs as will challenge but not overwhelm your child. Mix the cards and place them face down. Taking turns, each player turns over two cards. If they make a pair, the player keeps them and turns over another two cards until the cards turned over do not make a pair. When all the pairs have finally been claimed, the player with the greatest number of pairs is the winner. Make a separate set of cards to play addition, subtraction, multiplication and division "concentration."

➤ Redesign a checkers board for use in reinforcing multiplication facts. Make 32 new squares with a problem printed on each and tape them over the black squares. Play checkers the traditional way, except that before a player can move his piece, he must give the answer to the problem on the square he wants to move to. If he makes a mistake, he should be allowed to correct it and then move.

An alternative use of a checkerboard is to tape the numbers 1-12 to each set of disks. Follow the traditional rules of the game, with the following exception: When jumping another disk, a player must multiply the numbers involved before he can move. For instance if he jumps his "3" disk over his opponent's "6" disk, he must say, "Three times six equals eighteen." If a player wants to jump two disks, he must call out both problems before moving.

➤ Do you remember playing "Buzz" when you were learning multiplication tables? It can be played anywhere. Decide which facts you want to practice (for example, 4's), and one at a time, count off, beginning with "1." When you reach any number which is a multiple of 4 or which contains a 4, you must say "Buzz" instead of that number. (4's would go: 1, 2, 3, buzz, 5, 6, 7, buzz, 9, 10, 11, buzz, 13, buzz, 15, buzz, and so on.)

➤ Create a gameboard along the lines of the following one. Include a "Start," a "Finish" and label the spaces with instructions such as "Go ahead 3," "Go back 2," "Draw again," and "Lose a turn." Make game cards with math problems on them. To make the game more difficult, but also more interesting and useful, include lots of cards with a number missing other than the answer. For example, instead of 3 x 8 = __, try 3 x __ = 24 or __ x 8 = 24. Each player will need a marker, and you will need a

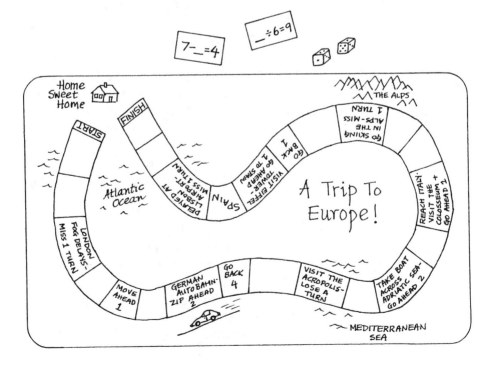

die or a spinner. The first player draws a card and must answer the problem correctly. Then he may spin (or roll) to see how far to move. It's up to the players to decide what the rule will be if a player gives an incorrect answer. He may lose his turn or keep trying until he gets the correct answer. Follow the instructions on the spaces as you move around the gameboard. The first player to reach "Finish" wins.

Understanding Place Value

As adults, we read large numbers all the time and think nothing of it. We often assume that our children can do the same. However, numbers become somewhat intimidating for many children once there are more than three digits and a comma or two.

First graders work on reading and writing numbers from 1 to 20. By the end of the year, they should be able to count to 50. Second graders learn all about numbers from 1 to 100, and how to count by 2's, 5's and 10's.

Third grade students should be able to read any number from 0 to 999. Third grade, then, is when students need to understand the concept of place value.

If your child has difficulty reading and writing three-digit numbers, you can help him by explaining that numbers are written in "periods" or groups of three. Each period is arranged in the same order: hundreds, tens, ones. There is a period for ones, another for thousands, another for millions, and so on.

If a number has only 3 digits, the first digit names how many hundreds, the middle digit names how many tens, and the third tells how many ones. For example, in the number "286," there are 2 hundreds, 8 tens and 6 ones.

Write down some three-digit numbers and ask your child to tell how many hundreds, how many tens, and how many ones there are in each. Then dictate numbers for him to write.

Fourth graders learn to read 6-digit numbers, saying the word "thousand" where the comma is, after the first period, and then reading the last period. Ask your child to read separately the numbers 578 and 163. Then write them as 578,163 and help your child read this new number. It is "five hundred seventy-eight thousand, one hundred sixty-three."

Write a few more six-digit numbers for your child to read. Before you ask your child to try writing 6-digit numbers, explain that there are only 3 spaces (1 period) in which to write the thousands. Go over the place value of the three spaces — hundred thousands, ten thousands and one thousands. It might help to draw 6 spaces at first, with a comma between the periods:

— — — / — — —

Then dictate a number, one period at a time. Remind your child that the word "thousand" indicates a comma.

Fifth graders learn 9-digit numbers up to 999 million. In the same way that you taught thousands, millions have 3 spaces only, one for hundred millions, one for ten millions, and one for one millions. The first comma is now the point at which we say "million." We say "thousand" at the second comma. For example: 123,456,789 is read "one hundred twenty-three million, four hundred fifty-six thousand, seven hundred eighty-nine."

Make up some nine-digit numbers for your child to practice on, and dictate similar numbers for him to write. Supply blanks, if necessary, at first.

— — — / — — — / — — —

Beware of numbers with zeros, especially when asking your child to write them. A number like "6 million, 23 thousand, 156" is often incorrectly written: 6,230,156. If this happens, cover the 6 and the 156 and ask your child to read the period, "230." Then ask him to think about how he can write just "23" using all three spaces. He will figure it out if you give him the chance to consider the possibilities.

Look for opportunities which provide a chance to practice number reading skills: in books, in the newspaper, on signs, on the odometer of your car.

Place Value Activities

➤ Each player gets a strip of paper and makes three dashes on the first line. The first player rolls a die and writes the number rolled in one of his three spaces. The second player does the same. Once each player has rolled once, everyone rolls again, writing the second number in one of the remaining two spaces. The object of the game is to see who can write the largest number. Therefore, the trick is deciding where to place the first two numbers. If you roll a low number, you would want to place it in the ones or tens place, hoping for a larger number on a later roll to put in the hundreds place. You can play this with as many players as you want. More spaces provide practice in reading larger numbers and understanding place value.

➤ Help your child try to imagine how big, or heavy, how many or how far some numbers are. It can be fun to try and find the right words to describe large quantities of something.

➤ It is also important that your child develop a sense of real meaning for large numbers. For example, make a point of watching for population signs as you drive into different towns and cities, and noting features such as size of buildings, the number of lanes in the main street, traffic, etc. Does your child know the population of the United States and the world? Try estimating the miles for a trip, and begin using comparisons.

Math Processes

Addition

Like reading numbers, addition is one of the basic math skills which you use all the time. Not only is addition important in finding a simple sum, but also in building other math skills.

Potential problem areas are learning to carry or regroup. This is usually first taught in the third grade. Look in your child's math text in order to give him problems at the correct level and in the right progression. If your child is still counting on his fingers, go back and work on addition facts. Not being certain of facts slows a child down and interferes with the ability to learn the new process.

A good place for addition practice is at the grocery store. Ask your child to keep track of what your groceries cost. Have him try to keep an exact account of money spent by adding the prices of the first two items together, and adding the price of the third item to the total of the first two, and so on. You can make it a game to see how close to the cash register total your child can come.

Subtraction

As carrying poses the greatest mystery in addition, so borrowing causes the most confusion in subtraction, especially when zeros are involved. Borrowing (a different type of regrouping) is usually introduced in the third grade.

Watch your child working out a math problem, at least until you have made sure he is executing the process correctly. Pay particular attention to problems with zeros in the top row. Many children will simply subtract the smaller number from the larger, regardless of which is on top.

If your child is having any difficulty, ask him to describe aloud the steps he is following as he works. This will help you discover the problem.

Show your child how to check his own subtraction problems to see if his answers are correct. Remember this trick?

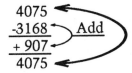

If these two numbers are the same, your answer is correct. If not, check your work carefully to discover the error.

Make a game board like the one below. The size is up to you. The only other materials you will need are paper and pencil for each player and two objects for tossing onto the board (poker chips, small bean bags, flat stones, etc.). Before the game starts, each player writes "100" at the top of his paper. Players take turns throwing the two poker chips onto the board and adding the two numbers. Each total is subtracted from the 100 on the paper. The player who reaches 0 first is the winner. (The game can be made more or less difficult by changing the size of the board or the distance from which the players have to throw the poker chips.)

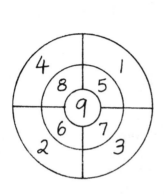

Multiplication

There are several common areas for mistakes in multiplication. Make a point of watching for them.

Zeros: Children sometimes treat a zero like a 1, or else they may ignore it.

Number placement: In 2-digit multiplication, be sure your child moves to the left one place before writing his second row of answers (figure A). Some people like to put in a zero as a *placeholder*. (figure B).

```
a. 463                          b. 463
   x21                             x21
   ───                             ───
   463                             463   The 0 placeholder
   926   Move over one place     9260   assures the second
   ────                          ────   row of answers will
   9723                          9723   be in the correct
                                        places.
```

In three-digit multiplication, the second row of answers shifts to the left one place and the third row of answers shifts over two places. In other words, *each answer should begin under the number you are multiplying by.* (Again, zeros may be used as placeholders.)

Careless Errors

★ Adding up the final answer incorrectly is often the result of sloppy work. If the rows of numbers are not lined up under each other correctly and neatly, the wrong numbers may get added together. If your child has this problem, encourage him to try turning his paper horizontally so that the lines go up and down. The lines will make columns to help him keep his ones, tens, hundreds, etc. lined up correctly.

★ Rushing often produces illegible numbers and a 3 might look like a 5, or a 6 might be mistaken for a 0.

★ After all the multiplying, some students forget to carry or simply add carelessly, throwing the whole answer off.

In math, close doesn't count. Math is an exact science and accuracy counts here more than almost anywhere else. Help your child learn to take the care necessary to be especially neat and accurate when he's dealing with numbers.

★ Encourage your child to check his answers. A fun method is an alternative method of multiplication sometimes called lattice multiplication. Set up the problem "37 x 95" as shown:

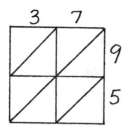

Multiply and write the answers to each fact in the proper spaces:

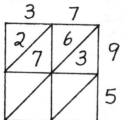
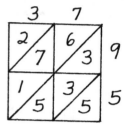

Add the diagonal sections, beginning with the bottom right. Carry when necessary, to the next lattice.

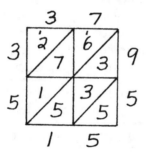

ANSWER = 3,515

★ Show your child how he can sometimes arrive at an answer by doubling (or tripling) instead of working out the problem the usual way. For example, to find the answer to 5 x 24, he can go to the fact 5 x 12 = 60, and double the answer. (Since 24 is 12 doubled, the answer to 5 x 24 will be double the answer to 5 x 12, or 120.) To find the answer to 8 x 15, he can go to 8 x 5 and triple the answer, since 15 is 5 tripled. (8 x 5 = 40, and 40 x 3 = 120.)

Division

 ake special care to watch for problems in the areas mentioned below.

Answer placement: Be sure the answer is written above the correct number. For instance in "12 ÷ 3", there are not four 3's in 1, so the answer "4" should not be written over the 1, but rather over the "2" in "12."

incorrect

$$\frac{4}{3)\overline{12}}$$

correct

$$\frac{4}{3)\overline{12}}$$

Zeros: Watch out for zeros. Children often ignore them at first.

incorrect

$$\frac{1\ 2}{3)\overline{306}}$$

correct

$$\frac{102}{3)\overline{306}}$$

Careless mistakes: As in multiplication, remind your child to write his numbers neatly and carefully as he works his problems. The possible results of sloppy work are obvious: A number is not "brought down," or is "brought down" twice and the wrong numbers are subtracted. Often numbers are simply subtracted incorrectly. Just one careless error and the whole problem is wrong!

Encourage your child to *self-check*. There is a nice way to check an answer to a division problem to find out whether or not it is correct: Multiply the answer (dividend) by the divisor, and you should come up with the subtrahend. If there is a remainder, it is added last of all.

a.
$$\frac{81}{9)\overline{729}}$$

$$\begin{array}{r} 81 \\ \times\ 9 \\ \hline 729 \end{array}$$

b.
$$\frac{23\ \text{r}\ 3}{4)\overline{95}}$$

$$\begin{array}{r} 23 \\ \times\ 4 \\ \hline 92 \\ +\ 3 \\ \hline 95 \end{array}$$

Once the problem has been done, a calculator can be used to check the answer. If your child's answer is correct, he'll feel confident about his ability to work out this type of problem. If his answer is not correct, he has the opportunity to go back, find his mistake and correct it while it is still fresh in his mind. This is a positive learning experience. In either case, knowing the answers are correct gives a feeling of pride in a job well done.

Math Strategies

Share any strategies or short cuts you use in figuring math problems. Introduce the concept of "Go to what you know." For example, if you were trying to solve 3 x 59, you could write the problem on paper and work it out. You could also stop and figure it out rather easily in your head, recognizing that 59 is just one less than 60, and the problem 3 x 60 is simply the fact 3 x 6 with a zero added — the answer is 180. To go back and figure out the answer to the original problem, 3 x 59, you would simply subtract one 3 from 180, and end up with 177.

By talking your way through this problem, allowing your child to see what you are doing, you can share a valuable way of looking at numbers. A child who can see how numbers relate learns to enjoy the challenge of making them work for him.

Your role is to show how math is used in your everyday life, talking through problems as you solve them. You needn't make a lesson out of every situation. Simply show by example when and how you work with numbers. It may be as you double a recipe's ingredients, figure out your car's gas mileage, determine how many square feet of tile you need to cover the kitchen floor, or estimate your monthly food bill. If the situation is right, include your child in the problem solving and encourage his help. Each time you do, you provide him with an opportunity to see math as an important and useful tool.

Fractions, Percents and Decimals

Fractions

We use fractions more than most of us realize. With your child, take a few minutes to consider how often we deal with fractions: cooking, measuring with a ruler, dividing things among a group, talking about the phases of the moon, making change, telling time and so on.

With a school-age child, it is important to use the proper terms for the top and bottom numbers in a fraction and encourage him to do the same:

$$\frac{1}{2} \quad \frac{\text{numerator}}{\text{denominator}}$$

The fraction 1/2 says that you are dealing with one part of a whole that has been divided into two equal parts.

Explain the "strange" fact that even though 6 is a larger number than 2, the fraction 1/6 means a smaller amount than 1/2. This is because the whole has been divided into more pieces, so each one is smaller. (Just ask any child if he'd rather have one piece of a pie cut in two pieces, or one piece of a pie cut in six pieces.)

Fraction Activities

➤ Help your child cut some circles, squares, and triangles of all different sizes out of construction paper. Then have him cut each in half, explaining that the two halves of an object must be equal. Explain, too, that though these halves are different shapes and sizes, they are all halves of their own original shapes. You can ask your child to go another step and cut the halves into fourths. Put the shapes "back together" to see how the parts work together, how they are related. Play with the pieces! Ask for 1/4 of the square or 1/2 of the triangle,

and have your child pick up the correct shape and
number of pieces.

➤ Make up problems like the following:

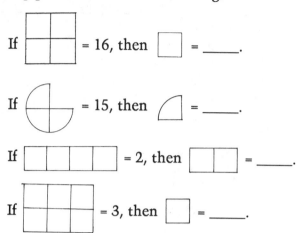

If ⬜ = 16, then ⬜ = ____.

If ◗ = 15, then ◿ = ____.

If ▭ = 2, then ▭ = ____.

If ⬛ = 3, then ⬜ = ____.

➤ Besides cutting a single thing into fractions, you will
also want your child to consider fractions of a group of
things. With a primary grade child, simply introduce
the idea. If I have 4 cookies and give you half of them,
how many will you get? If there are 20 carrot sticks in a
bowl and 1/4 of them are for your lunch, how many can
you eat? (Supply your child with 20 of some object —
marbles, beans, raisins, toothpicks — and have him
divide them into 4 equal groups.) How many in each
group? What is 1/4 of 20?

➤ With an upper elementary grade child, you can show
how multiplication, division and fractions work
together. Using beans, buttons, Matchbox cars, (any
countable objects), ask your child to figure out "What is
1/6 of 18? What is 1/5 of 25?" and so on. Help him see
the relationship between fractions and division facts.

1/6 of 18 equals   18 ÷ 6 which equals 3
1/5 of 25 equals   25 ÷ 5 which equals 5

Show him that he can then figure out 4/6 of 18, by
multiplying the answer to (1/6 of 18) by 4: 4 x 3 = 12.

➤ Using index cards, make a deck of "Fraction Concentration" cards. Spread the cards out face down on a table, and take turns turning over two of the cards, trying to match equivalent fractions (e.g. 1/2 and 2/4). If the two cards match, keep the pair and try again. If they don't, turn them face down again and let your opponent take his turn. The most common equivalent fractions are:

1/2, 2/4, 3/6, 4/8
1/3, 2/6
2/3, 4/6
3/4, 6/8
1/4, 2/8
1/1, 2/2, 3/3, 4/4

➤ Point out the fractional values of money. Teach your child that a quarter equals 1/4 of a dollar, because it takes 4 quarters to make a dollar. A dime is 1/10 of a dollar, because it takes 10 of them to make a dollar and so on. Play a money game where you "offer" to buy something for 1/4 of a dollar or 20 cents. Which "deal is best? Read the poem *Smart*, by Shel Silverstein in his book, *Where the Sidewalk Ends*. Your child will delight not only in the poem, but also in his ability to understand the humor.

➤ Help your child understand, too, the way we use fractions when reading a clock. There are 60 minutes in an hour, so 30 minutes equals a half-hour and 15 minutes equals 1/4 of an hour. Explain the expressions "quarter till" and "half past."

Percentages

If, as you watch a sport on television, your child asks you to explain percents (of passes completed, first serves in, and so on), take advantage of this prime opportunity to teach him about a concept he will encounter all his life. The suggestions below will also help you re-explain percentages to a child who is having difficulty understanding them as they have been presented in school.

Begin by explaining that percents are based on a set of 100. Different ratios or fractions can therefore be compared to a standard. Look at and discuss the figures below with your child. They each show a set of 100 squares, a certain number of which have been shaded.

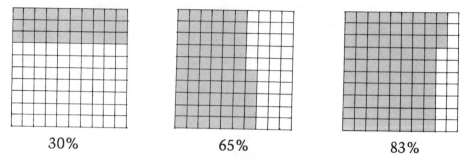

30%   65%   83%

A friend who teaches high school math suggests having students learn by heart, the most common percents. I would strongly recommend following the suggestion and have listed below the six most often used percents.

$$1 \text{ whole} = \frac{100}{100} = 100\% \qquad \frac{1}{2} = \frac{50}{100} = 50\%$$

$$\frac{1}{4} = \frac{25}{100} = 25\% \qquad \frac{3}{4} = \frac{75}{100} = 75\%$$

$$\frac{1}{3} = \frac{33}{100} = 33 \tfrac{1}{3}\% \qquad \frac{1}{10} = \frac{10}{100} = 10\%$$

You can introduce these easily enough with boxes of 100 squares like the ones above. Ask your child to make the boxes using graph paper. (Have him outline a 10 x 10 square and shade in the correct number of boxes.)

Another way to explain most of these percents is by comparing them to money, which is also based on a set of 100. Having 100 cents is having 100 percent of a dollar. Having a dime is the same as having 10 percent of a dollar; a quarter (25¢) equals 25 percent of a dollar; 50¢ equals 50 percent of a dollar; and 75¢ (three quarters) equals 75 percent of a dollar.

You can also describe these basic percents when dealing with amounts of food. Mention to your child when he has half of his sandwich left, "Fifty percent of your sandwich is left." Or try cutting apples (sandwiches, bananas, etc.) into fourths, showing that each quarter of the apple is 25 percent of it. Ask, "What percent of your apple is left? What percent have you eaten?"

Most important, point out the surprising abundance of percents around you. Make it a game to recognize them. Help your child write them down and talk about what they mean. Below are some places to watch or listen for percents.

★ Weather reports: "There is a 30 percent chance of rain today."

★ Sales tax: Explain that you pay a certain percent on every dollar you spend at the store.

★ Store sales on merchandise: "25 percent off all furniture." Look at advertisements together. "What will that sale do to the price of a bed that originally cost $500?"

★ Sports: During the tennis match, 60 percent of the player's first serves were good. In basketball, the player scored on 45 percent of his attempts. And so on.

★ Interest rates paid on loans and earned on savings. Encourage your child to start a savings account and help him figure out how much interest he will earn.

★ Grades in school: On a 10 problem test, each problem is worth 10 percent of the grade. Missing one problem would result in a grade of 90 percent.

Percentage Activities

➤ Your child can develop his own percentages about things around him. For example, have him jot down the colors of the first 10 cars which he sees drive by the house. Then ask him, "What percent of the cars were black? red? white?"

➤ Help your child keep track of commercials shown during an hour-long television program. He could time them, and determine what percent of the hour was devoted to commercials. Or he might note what kinds of commercials were shown, and afterwards, group them into categories and figure out what percent of commercial time was spent on beverage ads, clothing ads, car ads, and so on.

➤ Spend some time showing your child how sports statistics are derived. For instance, you could watch a basketball game together and help him keep a tally of the shots attempted and points scored by a particular player. Then show him how to figure out the percentage of baskets the player made. Help him figure out his favorite baseball player's batting average or a tennis player's percentage of good first serves.

Decimals

Decimals are simply another way of expressing fractions, using tenths or hundredths and sometimes even thousandths and ten thousandths. Certain decimals occur more often than others. Help your child get a feel for their values. For instance, .5 equals 1/2, and .25 equals 1/4. Other common decimals to look for are:

1/3 = .33 1/3   2/3 = .66 2/3   3/4 = .75

Explain that when reading decimals, we often use a short cut. Instead of saying "three-tenths" for .3, we might say "point three." Or instead of saying "forty-two hundredths," for .42, we often say "point four two."

Time

A friend of mine once described how her sixth grade son would run upstairs to his room and his digital clock to find out what time it was, because he couldn't read the regular clock in the living room! There may be digital clocks and watches everywhere, but there are also many of the "old" clocks around. Children still need to learn to tell time, and most should be able to tell time to the minute or second by the end of the third grade. (You might want to check your child's math text to see if this is also the expectation of his school.)

The best way to teach someone how to tell time is to play around with a clock with a second hand. Depending on your child's grade level, arrange the hands at times he should be able to recognize.

Show how each time the second hand has gone around once, a minute, or 60 seconds, has passed. Similarly, one complete revolution of the minute hand means 60 minutes, or one hour, has passed. Point out how we can count by 5's when reading a clock. Show, too, how to write time, using a colon (:) between the hour and minute. Explain the various time-related phrases such as "half past," "quarter past," and "quarter to," and the fact that a time may have more than one description. For example, 9:40 can be read "Nine forty," "Forty minutes past nine," or "Twenty minutes to ten."

Another part of understanding time involves seasons, months, days and weeks. Be sure your child understands these concepts. Help him feel comfortable using a calendar, and suggest he make his own!

Money

Even a preschooler knows what money looks like and that it is used to buy things. Beyond that, his comprehension of the concept behind the coins and bills is unnecessary. With a school-age child, an ideal way to explain coins and their values is to use 100 pennies, 10 dimes, 20 nickels, 4 quarters and 2 half-dollars. Show different ways to "make a dollar." Start with the 100 pennies in a pile. Give them to your child and ask him to count 5 pennies out. Trade him a nickel for them. Repeat until you have all the pennies and your child has 20 nickels. You want him to understand that he has the same amount of money, just in a smaller pocketful. Continue to show the relationship between the various coins.

Activities Involving Money

➤ Provide your child with a good supply of coins, and ask him to pick out and give you 21¢. Once he gives you the correct amount, ask him if he could have done it using a different combination of coins. Then ask for 63¢ or 47¢ and so on.

➤ Hand your child 3 dimes, a quarter, 2 nickels and 7 pennies, and ask him how much money he has. Try this with different amounts of money.

➤ Grocery stores provide countless ways to learn about money. When you return from the store with a bag of groceries, hand your child the cash register tape and have him locate and check off each item as you unpack it. Have him read aloud the price of each item, to practice reading amounts of money, and to become familiar with prices of everyday items.

➤ When you are shopping, ask your child to figure out which would be the most economical purchase: a 10-lb. bag of flour or two 5-lb. bags? Would it be less expensive to buy the larger box of cereal or two smaller ones which are on sale?

➤ If your store accepts coupons, encourage your child to clip coupons for items which you need. Let him find the items in the store and determine how much money you save.

➤ Help your child plan a meal. Ask him to estimate the costs, give him a budget, and let him shop for the food needed. Encourage him to use coupons and check the newspaper for specials. Then, cook it together.

Graphs

A graph is a valuable tool of communication; a helpful, visual method of presenting information. Graphs are used for many things. Consequently, we should be sure children understand how to read them and feel comfortable with the idea of making and using them.

There are three types of graphs most commonly encountered: bar, line and circle (pie). The bar graph below shows the number of ice cream cones purchased at an ice cream parlor one week. Help your child discover what is explained by each axis (the horizontal axis tells the days of the week; the vertical axis tells the number of cones sold, in increments of 5). Then help him answer the questions.

ICE CREAM CONE SALES

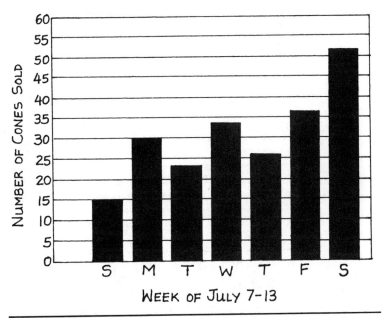

WEEK OF JULY 7–13

★ How many cones were sold on Friday?

★ On what day were the most cones sold?

★ On which day were the least number of cone sold?

★ How many more cones were sold on Monday than on Thursday?

★ What is the total number of cones sold during the week?

The line graph below shows Jim's progress in learning to jump rope. Look at the graph with your child before you have him answer the questions.

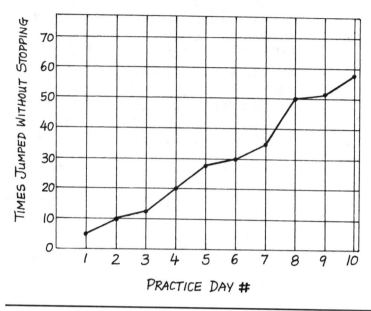

JUMPING ROPE - JIM

Y-axis: TIMES JUMPED WITHOUT STOPPING
X-axis: PRACTICE DAY #

★ How many jumps could Jim do on his first day of practice?

★ Did Jim get better? How does the line show that? What would the line look like if Jim got worse?

★ How much better did Jim do on Day #4 than on Day #2?

★ On what day did Jim jump 50 times without stopping?

The circle or pie graph on the next page tells how Carey spent her week's allowance.

★ How much money did Carey put into savings?

★ On what did she spend 80¢?

★ How much did Carey spend on ice cream?

★ How much allowance did Carey receive?

Encourage your child to make different types of graphs, measuring his growth, bird seed consumption per month, rainfall. Discuss which type of graph best illustrates the information collected.

Other ideas for either bar or line graphs are:

How Carey Spent Her Allowance

★ How many sit-ups or push-ups can you do?

★ How many hours of sleep do you get?

★ How much time do you spend watching T.V.?

★ How long does it take you to read out loud a particular page in your reading text?

★ How many math facts can you answer correctly before making a mistake?

Some ideas for making circle graphs would be:

★ Show how you spend the 24 hours of a normal school day. Include time spent sleeping, eating, at school, playing, doing work, and so on.

★ Show how you spent last week's allowance.

Many word processing programs involve the ability to make simple graphs. These are very helpful in encouraging students to take information from reports and present it visually. Encourage your child to keep track of temperature for science projects, voter turnout or congressional votes for social studies — all on computerized graphs. Children quickly learn which type of graph best displays their collected data.

Estimating

While math is considered an exact science, we often don't need to figure out precise totals. We may simply need to get an idea of the cost of something or of the total area of a room. To do this, we estimate. This is an extremely helpful skill for a child to learn.

Activities Involving Estimation

➤ Ask your child to estimate the width of a particular room. Then have him measure to get the exact width. The possibilities here are endless!

➤ Ask your child to estimate how many spoonfuls he'll eat before his bowl of cereal is gone, how many steps it takes to walk from the refrigerator to the table, how many peanuts he can hold in his hand, and so on. Encourage him to come up with more estimating activities of his own.

➤ Make an effort to "catch yourself" making estimates, and talk out your thinking as you do, so your child can see how you go about estimating something.
Have your child estimate the sizes of smaller objects: the length of a book, the length of a cassette tape, the width of his hand, the length of his arm or his hair, the circumference of his thigh or waist, and so on.

➤ Hand your child several objects and ask him to estimate the weight of each. Then have him weigh each on a scale to see how accurate his estimate was. Let him estimate the weight of different members of the family, the dog, his friends!

➤ Fill a jar with marbles (or a bucket with water), and ask your child to guess how many marbles are in the jar (or how many cups of water are in the bucket). He can then check his answer.

➤ As your child works out math problems, show him how estimating can help him quickly determine whether or not his answers are reasonable. For example, if he has the problem

$$5\overline{)3862}$$

he should estimate that 3,862 is close to 4,000, and 5 into 4,000 would be 800. Is his answer close to 800? If not, he will want to check it again.

Geometry Activities

When we hear the word "geometry," most of us immediately think of things like triangles, squares, right angles, protractors, and compasses. Rather than describe the basic concepts of geometry (which you can find in your child's math text), here are some fun, supplemental activities for you to try with your child. Each involves the skill of looking at the shape of an object, noticing its attributes, and how it is put together.

➤ Mix together in a bag or box, collections of objects such as small toy cars, leaves, buttons, old keys, and pens. Label blank sheets of paper by object type and ask your child to sort the objects into groups. Talk about the grouping. Help your child notice the different attributes of each group of items, and the similarities and differences within each group.

➤ Make a geoboard for your child. Take a piece of wood, approximately 6" x 6" square, and drill 3 rows of 3 holes. Space the holes 1" apart. Cut 9 pieces of doweling to fit the holes. Supply your child with an assortment of rubber bands and let him play with them on the geoboard. Ask him to try and stretch the rubber bands around the pegs to make different shapes. ("How many different triangles can you make? What is the biggest square you can make? Can you make a rectangle?" and so on.) Have him stretch rubber bands diagonally, across the top, bottoms, and side.

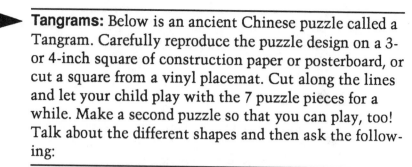

Tangrams: Below is an ancient Chinese puzzle called a Tangram. Carefully reproduce the puzzle design on a 3- or 4-inch square of construction paper or posterboard, or cut a square from a vinyl placemat. Cut along the lines and let your child play with the 7 puzzle pieces for a while. Make a second puzzle so that you can play, too! Talk about the different shapes and then ask the following:

★ Can you make a triangle using 2 pieces of the puzzle? 3? 4? 5? 6? all 7?

★ Can you make a sailboat using the puzzle pieces? a house? What other "pictures" can you design?

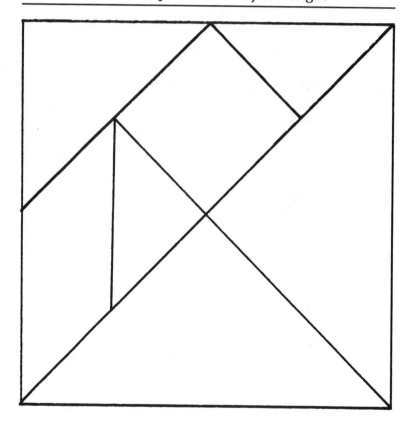

Creative
Problem-Solving

S I X

Creative Problem-Solving

reative problem-solving requires the use of both math and reasoning skills. Children can be taught various strategies which make problem-solving easier. These strategies provide a plan of attack and a concrete set of possible approaches to a problem. The best part is that the activities which teach the strategies are like riddles. They make it fun to think!

In addition to teaching their children the skills involved in problem-solving, parents need to explain that for many problems, there may be more than one way to find the answer. Flexibility in thinking is part of every strategy. Encourage your child to try using one approach to a problem, and if it isn't working, to try another. You want him to understand that there isn't always one right answer.

Introduce one problem-solving technique at a time. Use it until your child is comfortable with it, before introducing another.

Guess and Check

ometimes there is no logical approach to a problem. The only way to solve it is to guess an answer and if it is not correct, guess again, using the previous incorrect answer to guide you.

The conversation below shows how a parent might introduce this problem-solving strategy to his child.

Parent: I am trying to figure out a number. If I subtract 5 from it, then add 18, the answer is 22. Do you think the number could be 15?

Child: (looking confused) I don't know.

Parent: Well, let's try it out. If I subtract 5 from 15, what do I have?

Child: 10.

Parent: Right. Now if I add 18, what do I get?

Child: 28. That's too much.

Parent: If my guess of 15 was too big, what should we guess this time?

Child: Something smaller than 15. Let's try 8.

Parent: Check your guess and see what you end up with.

Child: O.K. 8 minus 5 equals 3, and 3 plus 18 equals 21. That's one less than 22.

Parent: So what should your next guess be?

Child: One more than my last guess — 9. Nine minus 5 equals 4, and 4 plus 18 equals 22. Nine is the answer!

Parent: Good work! Do you see how you solved the problem? You guessed an answer, checked it, and used what you found out to adjust your thinking and guess again. You can keep guessing and checking until you get the correct answer. Let's try one more.

As your child tries the problems below, encourage him to think out loud and follow the steps described above — *guess, check, adjust,* and continue until he finds the answer he's looking for. (See pages 179-182 for answers.)

★ 1a. I am thinking of a number. Multiply the number by 2. Then add 11. The answer is 39. What is the number?

★ 1b. What number is two times the sum of its digits?

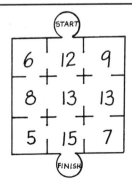

★ 1c. Find a path from start to finish with the sum of 74. You may only go through the open gates.

★ 2. The numbers in the big circles are found by adding the two numbers in the small circles. The example shows 14=6+8; 16=10+6; 18=8+10.

Example:

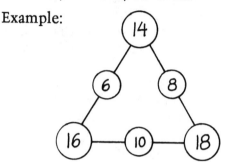

Find the numbers for the small circles in these two problems.

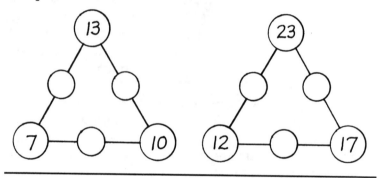

★ 3. For each problem, put the same number in the matching shapes to make true statements. Part "A" is done for you.

A.
$$\boxed{4} + \bigcirc{6} = 10$$
$$\boxed{4} \times \bigcirc{6} = 24$$

B.
$$\square \times \bigcirc = 40$$
$$\square + \bigcirc = 13$$

C.
$$\square + \bigcirc = 9$$
$$\square - \bigcirc = 5$$

D.
$$\square \div \bigcirc = 3$$
$$\square - \bigcirc = 8$$

Looking for Patterns

5, 4, 3, __, __

M S Y T Y S __

brother/sister   father/mother   uncle/_____

Can your child fill in the blanks above? It is simply a matter of looking for and discovering a pattern, a sequence, a relationship between things. Help your child notice how figures and numbers are related, how they change from one to another so that the pattern may be continued.

Parent: (Writes 3, 6, 9, __, __, __ on a piece of paper) Do you see any pattern in these numbers?

Child: The numbers go up by 3. (He might say they are multiples of 3 or you add 3 each time. There may be more than one way to describe a pattern. Any of these answers should be acceptable.)

Parent: Can you tell me what numbers would go in the blanks?

Child: Sure — 12, 15, and 18.

Parent: Right. What about this one? (Writes 1, 5, 6, 10, 11, __, __, __) Do you see a pattern here?

Child: Not really.

Parent: Well, take the first two numbers. How do you get from 1 to 5?

Child: You add 4.

Parent: O.K. And how do you get from 5 to 6?

Child: Add 1.

Parent: Now, what do you do to get from 6 to 10?

Child: Add 4 again.

Parent: And from 10 to 11?

Child: You add 1. So the pattern is: add 4, then add 1, right?

Parent: Right. Can you tell me the next three numbers now?

Child: 15, 16, 20.

Parent: Let's try one more. Look at these numbers. (Writes 1, 1, 2, 6, 24, __, __) Any idea about this pattern?

Child: It looks like you add 0 and then you add 1, but if you add 2, you don't get 6. That won't work.

Parent: But that was a good guess. How else can you get from 1 to 1?

Child: You could multiply 1 times 1.

Parent: Yes, then how would you get to 2?

Child: Multiply by 2. Then you multiply by 3 and you get 6. Multiply by 4 and you get 24. That works! You just multiply by one more each time.

Parent: Can you figure out the next two numbers? You can use this paper if you want.

Child: The next number would be 24 times 5, which is (he works it out on paper) 120, and then 120 times 6 which is 720.

Parent: Good work!

As your child tries to discover and complete the patterns below, remind him that if one pattern doesn't fit all the way, he should look for another.

★ 1. Write the next 3 numbers in each sequence:

a. 2, 4, 6, __, __, __

b. 1, 4, 7, 10, __, __, __

c. 1, 2, 4, 8, 16, __, __, __

★ 2. Three of the figures below are complete as given. Sketch the next two figures in each sequence.

a.

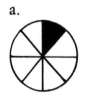

b.

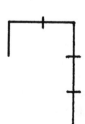

★ 3. Find a rule that gives the third number from the first two numbers. Fill in the blanks using the rule.

	a.	b.	c.
	8, 3, 11	5, 2, 10	10, 4, 6
	9, 5, 14	7, 5, 35	15, 7, 8
	4, 8, __	6, 4, __	19, 9, __
	6, __, 20	9, __, 45	7, __, 1
	__, 7, 19	__, 10, 30	__, 11, 12

Make a Systematic List

O n Saturday morning, you wake up without an alarm and linger under the warm covers a little while, smiling at the fact that you don't have to go to work. Once you get out of bed, however, you are overwhelmed by the tasks that lay before you on this, your "free day."

Should I take a shower first and then read the paper, or should I read and then shower? Should I sort the laundry and start the wash, or make breakfast? When will I get some exercise?

The alternatives in the order of action are endless. The choice is up to you. Making lists can be an effective way of visualizing the items with which you must deal in a great number of situations. The problems which follow help teach a child how to recognize all the alternative combinations which exist in a particular situation. Your job is to help your child learn to list alternatives in a systematic way.

Parent: Let's say you have the 3 letters: A, E, T. (Writes on paper.) Can you list all the 3-letter combinations that can be made using these letters? Give me one to start with.

Child: A E T.

Parent: (Writes each answer on the paper in an orderly list.) If I keep the A the first letter, what other combination can I make?

Child: A T E.

Parent: Now what if I start with the E. What will you get?

Child: E A T and E T A.

Parent: Good. What would you try next?

Child: Start with the T. You can make T E A and T A E.

The important job here is helping your child get organized in his approach to making a list of alternatives. Encourage him to exhaust all possibilities using one starting point before going on to a different one.

★ 1. At camp, these are the choices for supper.

Meat	*Potatoes*	*Vegetable*
steak	mashed	corn
trout	baked	green beans
		french fries

List the 12 different suppers a camper could choose if he eats one item from each group.

★ 2. Maggie was playing "Guess the Number" and gave these clues:

The number has 3 digits.
The digit in the hundreds place is greater than 7.
The digit in the tens place is less than 2.
The number is even.
What are the possibilities for the number?
Maggie gave this additional clue:
The sum of the 3 digits is 12.
Now what are the possibilities for the number?

Make a Drawing or Model

An architect makes drawings and constructs a model of the building he has designed. It is his method of testing his ideas by creating his building in miniature to determine if the real thing will work.

As you work with your child on the following activities, help him make drawings or build models which will make the solutions to the problems easier.

Remind him that there is no single correct drawing; rather there are a number of possible ways to illustrate the solution. You want to help your child find the simplest, clearest method of determining the answer. A child with a visual learning style will find this method particularly helpful.

★ 1. A fireman stood on the middle step of a ladder. As the smoke got less, he climbed up three steps. The fire got worse, so he had to climb down five steps. Then he climbed up the last six steps and was at the top of the ladder. How many steps were in the ladder?

★ 2. In a make-believe horse race between five famous horses:

    a. Citation finished one length ahead of Seattle Slew.

    b. Spectacular Bid finished ahead of Citation but behind Secretariat.

    c. Man-O-War finished four lengths ahead of Seattle Slew and one length behind Spectacular Bid.

    What was the finish place of each horse?

Eliminate Possibilities

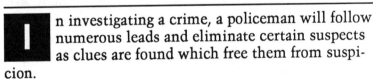 n investigating a crime, a policeman will follow numerous leads and eliminate certain suspects as clues are found which free them from suspicion.

A mechanic, trying to discover the reason for a car not running well, will check out various possible trouble areas until he discovers the problem.

Doctors perform different tests when trying to diagnose the cause of certain symptoms in a patient. Each negative result narrows down the possibilities and moves him closer to a diagnosis.

A legitimate method of dealing with problems, then, is eliminating possibilities. Have scratch paper ready for figuring, and encourage your child to use paper and pencil to experiment on, to list and eliminate possible solutions.

This strategy is similar to and begins like "Guess and Check." By applying the given criteria to guesses and keeping track of those which are not correct, your child can learn to narrow down the field of possibilities until only one remains.

★ 1. Jeff has less than 30 marbles. When he puts them in piles of three, he has no marbles left over. When he puts them in piles of two, he has one left. When he puts them in piles of five, he has one left. How many marbles does Jeff have?

★ 2. I am less than 100. I am an odd number. I am a multiple of 5. I am divisible by 3. The sum of my digits is an odd number. What number am I?

★ 3. Use the digits 3, 4, 8, and 9. Make two addition problems so each sum is greater than 150.

More Activities to Tease Your Brain!

Here are more problems to solve and puzzles to have fun with. Encourage your child to use different methods to solve them. You will have a better chance of helping him learn to approach and solve all kinds of problems if you can get him to verbalize why he is using a particular method.

➤ 1. Gabriel has 58¢ consisting of 9 coins. She does not have a half dollar. What coins does she have?

➤ 2. Fill in the last 3 numbers in the number pattern below. (Hint: Decide what operation was performed to get from each number to the next. Write down your findings and look for a pattern.)
10, 15, 12, 17, 14, __, __, __

➤ 3. Farmer McDonald raises ducks and cows. The animals have a total of 9 heads and 26 feet. How many ducks and how many cows does Farmer McDonald have?

4. Make this drawing. Place the numbers 1 to 7 in the circles to make the sum along each line 13.

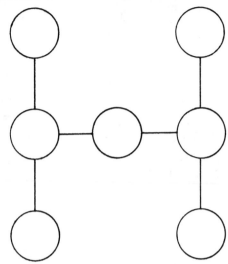

5. Use the digits 1 through 9 once each. Fill in the circles to make a sum of 999.

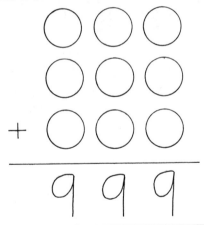

6. If Peter, Mike, Glen and Aaron each played one game of chess with each of the others, how many games were played in all?

7. Fill in the spaces in the figure on the next page with the numbers 1 through 9. Use each number only once to make a magic square which totals 15 when added in any direction.

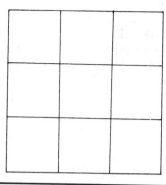

> 8. Use the numbers 1 through 9 to label the points on the triangle on the next page. Each side (4 points) must add up to 20.

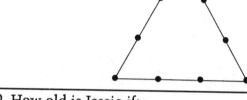

> 9. How old is Jessie if:
>   Mary is 5 years older than Taylor,
>   Taylor is 3 years younger than Jessie,
>   and Mary is 15 years old?

> 10. Arrange the numbers 1 through 8 so that no consecutive numbers are touching, either on a side or on a corner.

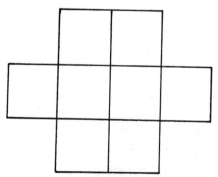

> 11. How many apples did you buy if:
>   Apples cost 10¢ each or 3 for 25¢,
>   you paid for the apples with a $1 bill,
>   and you received 15¢ change.

12. I have a number. If I add it to 367, I get the same answer as I do when I subtract it from 663. What is my number?

13. How many games did our basketball team win if we played 18 games, and we won 4 more games than we lost?

14. If a hamburger and a milk shake cost $1.50, and two hamburgers and a milk shake cost $2.40, how much does a milk shake cost?

15. Does "18 H. on a G.C." mean anything to you? It's simply a number puzzle, and stands for "18 holes on a golf course." Here are a few more puzzles like "18 H. on a G.C.":
   a. 24 H. in a D.
   b. 9 P. in the S.S.
   c. 26 L. in the A.
   d. 4 S. in the Y.

Answers to Problems

Guess and Check (pages 169 and 170)

1. a. 14
    b. 18
    c.

2.

3.

B.

$$\boxed{8} \times \textcircled{5} = 40$$

$$\boxed{8} + \textcircled{5} = 13$$

C.

$$\boxed{7} + \textcircled{2} = 9$$

$$\boxed{7} - \textcircled{2} = 5$$

D.

$$\boxed{12} \div \textcircled{4} = 3$$

$$\boxed{12} - \textcircled{4} = 8$$

Looking for Patterns (pages 172 and 173)

1.   a. 8, 10, 12
   b. 13, 16, 19
   c. 32, 64, 128

2.   a.

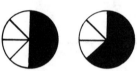

     b.

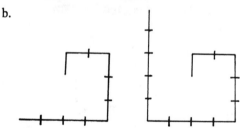

3.   a. 12; 14; 12
   b. 24; 5; 3
   c. 10; 6; 23

Making a Systematic List (page 175)

1.   steak, mashed potatoes, corn
   steak, mashed potatoes, green beans
   steak, baked potato, corn
   steak, baked potato, green beans
   steak, french fries, corn
   steak, french fries, green beans
   trout, mashed potatoes, corn
   trout, mashed potatoes, green beans

trout, baked potato, corn
trout, baked potato, green beans
trout, french fries, corn
trout, french fries, green beans

2.   a.   800, 802, 804, 806, 808
              810, 812, 814, 816, 818
              900, 902, 904, 906, 908
              910, 912, 914, 916, 918
     b.   804 or 912

Making or Using a Drawing or Model (page 175)

1.   9 steps in the ladder
2.   1st place: Secretariat
      2nd place: Spectacular Bid
      3rd place: Man-O-War
      4th place: Citation
      5th place: Seattle Slew

Eliminating Possibilities (page 176)

1.   Jeff has 21 marbles
2.   45
3.   83 + 94 (=177)
     93 + 84 (=177)

More Activities to Tease Your Brain (pages 176 - 178)

1.   1 quarter, 1 dime, 4 nickels, 3 pennies
2.   19, 16, 21
3.   5 ducks, 4 cows
4.

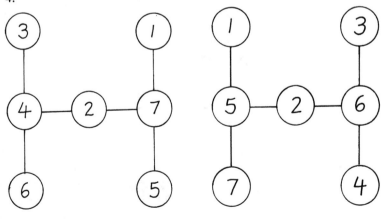

5. Five "basic" solutions are possible:

195	159	194	139	169
476	462	267	286	287
+328	+378	+538	+574	+543
999	999	999	999	999

Many variations of these are possible simply by moving numbers around within a column.

6. 6 games

7.

4	9	2
3	5	7
8	1	6

8.

9. Jessie is 13 years old.

10.

	6	4	
2	8	1	7
	5	3	

11. 10 apples

12. The number is 148.

13. Our basketball team won 11 games.

14. A milk shake costs 60 cents.

15. a. 24 hours in a day
b. 9 planets in the solar system
c. 26 letters in the alphabet
d. 4 seasons in the year

Fun with Science

S E V E N

Fun with Science

During the summer following fourth grade, Donna and her cousin, Cindy, spent hours playing around the pond across the road from Donna's house in rural Kansas. The girls, like most children, loved digging in the mud and looking for various pond creatures.

One day, the girls discovered masses of jelly-like polliwog eggs. Excited by their find, they ran home for a bucket in which to put some of the eggs. Not only did they have polliwog eggs, but there were also tadpoles at various stages of development. Many had fat bodies and long tails. Some were even beginning to grow legs. The girls were fascinated.

The next morning Donna hurried to the bucket, only to find that almost all of the smallest tadpoles were missing. "That's disgusting!" she thought when she realized that the larger tadpoles had eaten the smaller ones. Cannibals! Her mother suggested she try getting some more, but this time, separate them by size. "Put all the eggs in one container, the little tadpoles in another, and the big ones in another," she said. This division of tadpoles solved the problem, and Donna and Cindy spent long hours during the next month or so, following the growth of the tadpoles.

This "summer of the tadpoles" happened over twenty years ago, but the experience remains clear in Donna's mind. Children, if given the freedom to try and test "theories" tend to want to know the how's and why's of all kinds of things. The more children discover, the more they question, the more they search for answers.

It is unfortunate that so many of our children are taught "textbook science," where they *read about* numerous scientific concepts and methods, but are asked to try out very few. As parents, there are a number of steps we can take to try and change this situation. We can work with our schools and teachers to incorporate more hands-on experimentation into the curriculum, and we can work individually with our children to develop a more positive attitude toward science.

Improving Science in Your Child's School

"Every now and then, I'm lucky enough to teach a class in kindergarten or the first grade. Many of these children are curious, intellectually vigorous, ask provocative and insightful questions and exhibit great enthusiasm for science. When I talk to high school students, I find something different. They memorize 'facts.' But, by and large, the joy of discovery, the life behind those facts, has gone out of them. They're worried about asking "dumb" questions; they're willing to accept inadequate answers; they don't pose follow-up questions; the room is awash with sidelong glances to judge, second-by-second, the approval of their peers. Something has happened between first and 12th grade, and it's not just puberty. I'd guess that it's partly peer pressure not to excel (except in sports); partly that the society teaches short-term gratification; partly the impression that science or math won't buy you a sports car; partly that so little is expected of students; and partly that there are so few role models for intelligent discussion of science and technology or for learning for its own sake."

This description by Carl Sagan, author of *Cosmos* and creator of the award-winning T.V. science series by the same name, presents a sad picture of our society's attitude toward science. It also offers an explanation for American high school students scoring so much lower in all areas of math and science than their counterparts in other areas of the world.

The solution to the problem must come from school and the home. Parents need to ask why it is that many elementary schools invest in specialists to teach physical education and music, but don't consider adding a specially-trained science teacher to the staff? If parents would take the time to present a strong case for better science programs in elementary and middle schools, the results could be impressive and extremely valuable, for students and society as a whole.

Even the most diligent elementary school teacher can't be expected to provide a terrific science program if she has little support from others. If your school can't or won't add a science specialist to the staff, encourage the administration to provide some good in-service training for its teachers.

Encouraging Science at Home

"What's wrong with the garbage disposal?"

"I'm not sure. My guess is that the pipe under here is clogged. If you'll get me a wrench, we'll see if I'm right."

"Where does the water come from when you flush the toilet?"

"Here. We'll look under the lid of the tank and see what happens."

By presenting a good role model and taking the time to help a child find answers, a parent can encourage him to question, formulate hypotheses and test them. The situations above invite parents to encourage curiosity and investigation. The more you explain, demonstrate and let your child discover answers for himself, the more he will appreciate science.

Put together a "home science kit" which makes equipment readily available and encourages a child to question, test, investigate. Items in the kit might include paper, charcoal (for rubbings), magnifying glass, tweezers, a canning jar with a screen lid or with holes punched, a few odd-sized plastic containers and/or an egg carton. For older children, there might also be a funnel, tubing for siphoning, a battery cell and some wire, plus small lights and a bell or buzzer. A child who shows genuine interest might make good use of a small microscope with slides, slide covers, and basic stains for making specimens.

Consider buying a building set that includes pulleys, wheels, and gear wheels. More sophisticated sets are made for older children. Playing with these items teaches many things that books or words cannot. Invest in a copy of *The Way Things Work*, by David Macauley. It makes the world around us come alive.

The next time you find yourself about to discard a non-functioning clock, telephone, or other small appliance, consider turning it over to your child to tinker with, take apart, salvage gears and other parts from. Help him dismantle the object and see how it was put together. Then, invite him to try to repair it or invent something new.

Make a point of watching science programs on television together. *National Geographic* specials, *NOVA, COSMOS, 3-2-1 Contact* and shows offered on the Discovery Channel and PBS introduce the scientific approach while studying a terrific variety of fascinating phenomena. Point out the different science-related careers presented in these shows.

Try to visit science museums, especially "hands-on" museums, where children are encouraged to touch and play with equipment and exhibits. Marinelife aquariums offer an opportunity to see huge sea mammals only inches away through glass and to touch creatures such as sea anemones and horseshoe crabs. Visits to facilities like these expand a child's knowledge of and appreciation for the world around him.

Lastly, when you and your child are unable to solve a problem through your own investigations, make a point of heading for the encyclopedia or library to find the answers you need.

Building Observation Skills

Would your children have trouble recognizing their own dog? their own desks at school? Probably not. What about their own peanuts? To help children appreciate the smallest of differences in things which may at first glance appear similar, give every member of the family his own peanut, a piece of paper and a pencil. Ask each person to spend a few minutes "getting acquainted" with his peanut, noting on the paper, any observations he makes about his particular peanut. When everyone is finished, collect the peanuts and mix them up in a bowl. Ask each person to find his own peanut.

When all the peanuts have been identified, ask family members if they thought the task was difficult. Talk about which observations were most helpful in identifying one's own peanut. Add additional notes which would be helpful in identifying each peanut.

Now, mix the peanuts in the bowl again, and exchange pieces of paper. This time, each person is to find another person's peanut, using that person's notes. Talk about which observations were clearest and most helpful.

Keeping Records

Many children like to graph or record their findings. Somehow this confirms what they do and observe. To encourage this type of activity, provide a special notebook to record results and observations. If your child has access to a computer, he might want to explore graphing his results, first deciding whether a bar, line or pie graph is most appropriate. Older children can learn how to set up a page to include the various stages of scientific investigation:

★ state the question

★ make a hypothesis

★ consider the variables to be controlled and which one to vary

★ plan how to test

★ list materials needed

★ collect data and record observations accurately

★ compare findings with the hypothesis

★ state a conclusion

Nature: It's Right Outside Your Door

Nature Walks

One of the easiest and most enjoyable ways to nurture curiosity and share Nature is by taking "exploration walks." No equipment is needed, no special season or time of day required. All that is necessary is an unhurried attitude of pleasant anticipation of things to be discovered.

Encourage your child to lead the way, and go slowly. Help him learn that the most interesting things are often small and out of sight. Squat or kneel down and poke in the dirt, look into bushes, carefully lift rocks to discover what lives underneath. Be sure to replace the rock afterwards so as not to disturb the world of the creatures which live there.

Gently take apart different kinds of flowers and ask your child to notice similarities and differences. Cut into a mushroom to see how it is made. Watch different types of insects going about their business. Hold a piece of paper under a shrub and shake the plant to see what falls onto the paper.

Have your child choose a tree in your yard or neighborhood to study. Encourage him to make a special notebook about the tree including drawings and notes about its changes through the different seasons. Have him watch for any animals or other plants which may live in or off of "his" tree.

You might want to invest in one or more field guides. Select books which are not overly technical, but which offer enough information to help identify most of the living things you are apt to encounter on your walks.

Lastly, pass on to your child an appreciation of all living things. No matter how unappealing some creatures might seem, each living thing plays a role in nature. Consider together how the destruction of just one form of life, can endanger the survival of the others.

Insects

Insects are easy to study because they are so readily available! As you discover different insects (live ones you see on your walks or even dead ones you find on the grill of your car), ask questions which require looking carefully and noticing how insects are alike and how they are different. As you look together at insects, ask questions like the ones below.

★ Can you tell how many main parts an insect's body has?

★ How many legs does an insect have?

★ Do insects have wings?

★ Do you see the "feelers" on the insect's head? Do you know another name for them?

★ I wonder how insects protect themselves. Can you think of different ways?

★ Can insects be harmful? How?

Nature Activities

➤ Help your child start an insect collection. Record time, place, weather conditions where each specimen was found. Draw an illustration to accompany the data.

The life cycle of the beetle: Observe the entire life cycle of little black beetles, by starting with some mealworms which can be purchased at a pet store. Place several layers of uncooked oats or bran in a glass jar with the mealworms. Sprinkle with water and add a few pieces of raw potato or apple. It will take several weeks for the mealworms to develop into beetles. Then the beetles will lay eggs, the eggs will develop into mealworms, and as long as the environment is maintained and food provided, the cycle will continue.

Investigating ants: Studying ants can provide a great starting point for some scientific observation. If you accompany your child at first, he will more than likely continue later on his own. Questions like the following can help rouse his curiosity.

★ Find an ant and watch it. Can you see the 3 separate parts of its body? (If you have a magnifying glass, you can get a closer look.)

★ How many legs does an ant have? Which part of its body are the legs connected to? Does the ant move quickly or slowly?

★ Look at the ant's antennae. How often does it clean them? How does it clean them?

★ What do two ants do when they meet each other?

★ Can an ant carry something larger than itself? Can you find two ants working together to carry one large thing? (You might set some different size crumbs of bread nearby and see what the ants do with them.)

★ Follow the ants to see where they are going. Do they go in different paths or follow the same one coming and going?

★ What happens if you rub your finger across the earth in front of an ant?

★ What does the ant do if you put some objects down in front of it?

★ Carry some ants away and put them down again. Can they find their way home?

Making an ant farm: If your child shows interest in ants, suggest making an "ant farm" together. This can be done quite easily using two squares of glass or Plexiglas and four strips of wood (1/4" wide) to separate the glass.

★ Lay one square of glass on the table and glue the four strips along the edges. (You will need to have drilled two holes, several inches apart, in one of the strips of wood. These openings will be used to supply the ants with food and water.)

★ Fill inside the square with sifted earth from an ant hill, leaving the center clear, and making paths from the two openings to the center. Plug the two holes in the strip of wood with cotton.

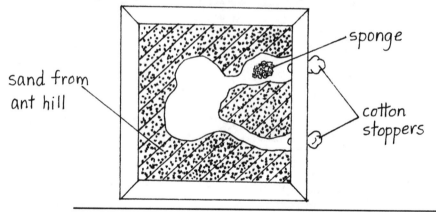

sponge

sand from ant hill

cotton stoppers

★ Locate an ant colony. Check underneath logs, stones and debris. Look for a queen ant, usually much larger than the worker ants. You will need a queen in order to observe the entire life cycle. Gently but quickly scoop up the queen and a few workers with a shovel and place them in a plastic bag. As you transfer them to the ant farm, have someone ready to place the second square of glass on top of the wood strips to seal the ants inside! Secure the square with adhesive tape.

★ Insert a moist bit of sponge into one of the holes, and small bits of food into the other. (You can feed ants tiny pieces of bread, cookies, or honey.) Be sure to keep the holes plugged except when re-moistening the sponge or adding food!

★ Cover the top piece of glass with a piece of cardboard, taped along one side. This hinged cover will create the dark atmosphere the ants need to live normally, but will allow you to lift and observe the ants from time to time. Talk about how these ants live and work together.

★ A child who is especially fascinated by insects might want to consider joining Y.E.S., the Young Entomologists' Society, which sends out a newsletter to its school-age members. For more information, your child can write: Y.E.S., International Headquarters, 1915 Peggy Pl., Lansing, MI 48910.

Plant Activities

There are lots of activities and experiments which can help children learn about plants, how they grow, how they transport water from roots to leaves, how they reproduce, and so on.

➤ Add red or blue food coloring to half a glass of water, the darker the color, the better. Cut the bottom three inches off a piece of celery, setting the stalk in the colored water. Check back in several hours. The color will have moved up through the stalk and into the leaves. Cut across the stalk so that your child can see a cross-section of the veins which carry water up the stalk.

➤ Give your child a plant for his room. Explain that, unlike animals, green plants are able to make their own food through a process called photosynthesis. Ask him if he knows what a plant needs in order for photosynthesis to occur (sunlight, water, soil, air, chlorophyll).

Explain that plants and animals are partners. Plants use carbon dioxide from the air and produce oxygen. Animals breathe the oxygen the plants produce, and in turn make carbon dioxide for the plants to use.

Older children can draw the plant-animal oxygen cycle to see how living things need to interact.

Start several plants from seeds. Once they have grown to about 2" in height, help design an experiment to determine the effect of light on the growth of the plants. Choose different locations for each plant, from direct sunlight to darkness (set one in a closet). Guess or *hypothesize* what will happen. Keep accurate notes and observations on the plants, measuring their growth and noting changes in the leaves. Explain the importance of keeping all other conditions the same (water and temperature), and varying only the amount of light (single variable). Talk about why this kind of control is a critical aspect of scientific investigation.

In the spring, start growing some flowers and vegetables inside. Remind your child to use what he learned from the experiment above to provide the best growing conditions possible.

On a walk, see how many different kinds of leaves you can find. At home, make leaf rubbings by rubbing a crayon over a piece of paper with a leaf underneath. Label the leaf drawings, noticing the difference in shapes, colors, edges and vein patterns.

If you have space for a garden, let your child plan a small garden of his own. He can plant his own vegetables and flowers and care for them. If you don't have a yard, consider growing "terrace tomatoes." The planning stage can bring in lots of math skills, and the caring stage involves lots more science — fertilizer, water, parasites, etc.

Spore prints: Look for a fresh mushroom in a damp, wooded area. Help your child carefully remove the stem and set the mushroom on a piece of white paper. Place two pencils underneath the edges of the mushroom to keep it from touching the paper. Leave overnight. In the morning, when your child lifts the mushroom cap from the paper he should find an intricate print on the paper, created by the thousands of tiny spores or mushroom seeds which have fallen during the night.

➤ Look at the trimmings of a wandering jew, coleus, Swedish ivy or Boston fern. Note the colors in the leaves. Cut the trimmings into 1/2" pieces and place them in a pot with about 1" of water. Simmer, covered, for 20 minutes or so. While the leaves are simmering, ask your child to hypothesize what color will simmer out of the trimmings. Then get out some safe kitchen "chemicals" and do some testing. Smell and taste some of the following: baking powder and soda, a clear soft drink, pickle juice, salt, sugar, and vinegar.

After the 20 minutes have passed, remove the trimmings and look at the water. Introduce the word pigment if your child does not know it. (Pigment is what gives something its color. The pigment which makes plants' leaves green is called chlorophyll. There are also pigments in skin, hair, the iris of one's eyes, and so on.)

Now try mixing a small amount of plant juice with the different chemicals tested earlier. Note what happens with each mixture.

➤ Grow your own bean sprouts using a canning jar, the metal rim, and gauze in place of the lid. Cover a layer of alfalfa or mung beans (you can purchase them at a health food store) with one to two inches of water. Leave overnight in a dark place. In the morning, drain the water out, rinse with fresh water and drain again. Set the jar in a dark place. Fill it with fresh water and drain it out, twice a day for 3 or 4 days. (This is the hardest part — remembering to rinse and drain.) It won't be long before the bean sprouts will be ready to eat in sandwiches and salads!

As you both follow the progress of the sprouts, look in books for information on seeds, sprouting, and the formation of root systems.

Astronomy

E ven when we know better, we say, "The sun rises in the east," as if it's the sun that does the moving. Here's an activity to try some evening, after it's grown reasonably dark, which will help dispel some of the widely held "myths" about the earth's relationship to the sun.

Set a bright lamp on a table in the middle of the room and remove the lamp shade. Imagine that the lamp is the sun. Let your child be the earth and slowly move (revolve) around the sun in a path or orbit.

Then, ask him to stand in one spot and turn very slowly around in a counterclockwise direction. Explain that this is how the earth turns or rotates. When he is facing the sun, it is day on that side of the earth which faces the sun. As he turns, he sees less of the sun, until finally his back is toward the sun. This is night. As he continues around, it becomes day again. Finally let him try combining the two movements — slow rotation as he revolves around the sun.

Of course, the next step is to venture outside on a clear night to look at the heavens. Although a telescope is nice to have, it's not a must and a pair of binoculars works well. If you don't have binoculars, try looking at the stars through cardboard tubes from paper towels or toilet tissue; they help eliminate peripheral lights and allow you to see the stars more easily. Take time to search the sky for some of the celestial bodies you've studied in books. Try to comprehend the enormity of the universe. Imagine aloud the possibility of life on other planets. It's a truly baffling and almost humbling experience when you begin to understand how very small we are, and how vast the universe is.

Astronomy Activities

➤ Our solar system is made of the sun and the nine planets which revolve around it. They are, in order from the sun: Mercury, Venus, Earth, Mars, Jupiter, Saturn, Uranus, Neptune, and Pluto. Invite your child to create his own solar system in his bedroom. Planets and a sun (made by different size balloons covered with papier-mache and painted) can be suspended from the ceiling. Your child might add spaceships and satellites. Let him use his imagination!

Make a sky clock: With a little preparation, you and your child can learn to tell time at night using the Big Dipper. First, duplicate the two clock parts shown below.

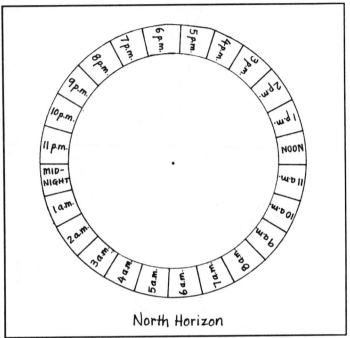

North Horizon

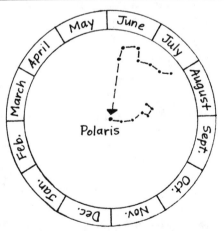

Polaris

Glue the parts to posterboard and cut around the outside of each. Use a brass paper fastener to attach the month dial to the hour dial, centering carefully. Be sure to mark "North Horizon" on the bottom of the hour dial, as shown.

Take the clock and go outside on a clear night. Face north and locate the Big Dipper. Hold the clock so that the words "North Horizon" are at the bottom. Rotate the month dial until it matches the position of the Big Dipper in the sky. The approximate time can be determined by matching the current month with the clock time adjacent to it.

➤ Make a moon calendar to help a child understand that the moon's changing shape is the result of its revolving around Earth. It needn't be a regular calendar format. Your child could make one long row of boxes to mount on his wall. Each night draw the moon's profile on the calendar noting the date in each box. Help your child label each drawing using the appropriate terms to describe the phase shown (crescent, gibbous, new moon, old moon, half-moon, full moon, first quarter, last quarter). Discuss the terms "waxing" and "waning."

➤ An illustrated study guide of the phases of the moon with activity ideas is available for $1.50 from Jenny Pon, Abrams Planetarium, Michigan State University, East Lansing, MI 48824.

➤ Visit a planetarium. (Children under 5 are often frightened in a planetarium.) Check into borrowing a home telescope for a night or visiting a large night-viewing astronomy lab at a nearby college.

➤ Your child can send for a step-by-step guide to becoming an amateur astronomer by sending $3 for "Astronomy as a Hobby" to: Astronomical Society of the Pacific, Hobby Packet Dept. 1290 24th Ave., San Francisco, CA 94122.

The Amazing Human Body

Children love to learn about how the human body works because it is a subject they can relate to on a personal level. With a young child, nurture his interest in health and basic physiology by drawing his attention to interesting phenomena. For instance, the next time your child cuts himself and bleeds, ask him if he knows how the bleeding stops. Explain that the blood contains special substances which work to form a clot. Make a point of noting together the changes in the wound as it heals.

When your child has a fever, ask him if he knows why his body is so hot. Does he understand that the heat is one way his body tries to fight invading disease cells? This is one reason doctors tell parents not to rush with the Tylenol to lower a child's temperature unless the child is uncomfortable or the fever is dangerously high. The body may be able to handle the situation if we will let it use its own built-in defense system.

Ask your child to imagine what his body would look like if he had no skeleton. Can he explain the various functions of the bones in his body? (They support and protect the body's organs and tissues and allow him to walk, run, and move in different ways.) Does he know how many bones he has in his entire body (206) and where the 3 smallest bones are located (in the ear)? Children in grades 3 and up love learning the names of the bones in the body. It gives them a great sense of accomplishment to "rattle off" the scientific names for the human skeletal structures. Does your child know what is inside his bones (marrow)? What is manufactured in the bone marrow (blood cells)? What kinds of food contribute to strong, hard bones (foods rich in calcium, such as milk, cheese, and beef)?

Help your child measure his pulse, figuring out approximately how many times an hour his heart beats. How many times a day would that be? How many times in one year does his heart beat? Have him squeeze a ball in a steady rhythm (aim for approximately one squeeze per second) until his hand muscles get tired. It should give him an appreciation for his heart, which essentially does the same thing, minute after minute, hour after hour, day after day...

Preadolescence: A Period of Questions and Change

A preadolescent child becomes more aware of how the human body changes during a lifetime. He is more sensitive to the aging he sees taking place in his parents and grandparents. The preadolescent begins to take an interest in how his own body serves him. Exercise, diet and hygiene become more important as he sees that these factors affect his physical performance and his personal appearance. He also has to deal with his body beginning to change in ways over which he has no control.

By the time a child reaches the upper elementary grades, he has likely come in contact with or knows of students who abuse drugs and alcohol. Substance abuse must be taken seriously in both rural and urban communities. In addition to talking about drugs, alcohol, and tobacco at home, parents need to support drug education in their children's schools. These programs are very effective in helping children learn to be assertive and to deal with peer pressure as well as in educating them on the dangers of drugs.

All preadolescents have doubts and fears concerning the changes they are experiencing. They have a lot of questions for the parent who will listen respectfully and answer seriously. For many parents, discussing sex and substance abuse with their children is something they would rather avoid. Yet, considering the near-epidemic of substance abuse, teenage pregnancy, venereal diseases and AIDS, discussions which promote a healthy understanding of how one's body functions and how it can be protected are vital. The sooner the lines of communication are opened and the more comfortable a child is in talking with his parent about virtually any topic, the better.

Caring for Our Environment

The work for environmental awareness starts at home. It's crucial that we work on raising children who understand the need to take care of their environment. We can help them enormously by making recycling a fact of life, not a choice. We need to recycle, not only because our landfills are rapidly filling up, but for the simple reason that the attitude which allows such flagrant waste of resources is arrogant and unnecessary. Consider these statistics:

★ Every three months, we throw away enough aluminum cans to rebuild our entire commercial air fleet.

★ Each Sunday, 500,000 trees are made into newspapers that aren't recycled.

The needed changes in attitude toward the environment will come about only if parents make an effort themselves to recycle and to encourage community involvement in this problem. Our children learn by our example. Encourage them to approach neighbors about saving aluminum cans, or arrange to pick up neighbors' bundled newspapers once a week for recycling if you are lucky enough to have a facility nearby which will accept them. Help your child understand also, the need for creating and maintaining a market for recycled materials. Without a market, recycling doesn't work.

If there is not yet mandatory recycling in your state, encourage your child and/or his entire class to write letters to state representatives about the need for it.

Looking at the Whole Earth

Beyond our homes and local communities is a world which is suffering because of the mismanagement of its resources. For very obvious reasons, it is important that our children become involved in and learn about remedying the situation. Among the very real concerns are acid rain, radioactive wastes from nuclear power plants, and global warming.

If you and your children will start researching the subject of environmental protection, I think you will find it both interesting and rewarding. Watch for articles in the newspaper and reports on television which concern environmental issues. Discuss them, and encourage your children to send for information, do some research and get involved in working for needed changes.

There are a great many organizations which work to protect the earth and its resources. There are also publications which provide information about caring for the planet. The following are just a few you and your children might want to contact for more information about the problems that exist, what can be done about them, and how to get involved.

★ Environmental Defense Fund
National Headquarters
257 Park Avenue South
New York, NY 10010
or call EDF's hotline at 1-800-CALLEDF
for information about recycling.

★ Public Affairs Office
U.S. Environmental Protection Agency
Washington, D.C. 20036

★ National Clean Air Coalition
530 7th Street SE
Washington, D.C. 20003

★ The Acid Rain Foundation
1630 Blackhawk Hills
St. Paul, MN 55122

★ Contact your state's Office of Pollution Control and Ecology for information on recycling in your area.

★ Write your governor, state senators and state representatives and ask about environmental monitoring in your state. In some states, programs have been developed which use volunteers to monitor regularly.

★ Keep America Beautiful
9 West Broad Street
Stamford, CT 06902
(Offers a number of free informational pamphlets, and a list of others provided for a minimal fee; can tell you who to contact about KAB program in your state.)

★ National Wildlife Federation
1412 16th Street NW
Washington, D.C. 20036-2266
(publishes several magazines for children)

★ Sierra Club
530 Bush Street
San Francisco, CA 94108

★ National Audubon Society
950 Third Avenue
New York, NY 10022

★ Ohio Alliance for the Environment
445 King Avenue
Columbus, OH 43201
(Ask for the information sheet entitled: "Focus on the Issue: Understanding Ohio's Solid Waste Crisis.")

★ Connecticut Fund for the Environment
152 Temple Street
New Haven, CT 06510
(Send $5 for "Household Hazardous Waste." This 1987 guide identifies hazardous substances in household products and describes how to best dispose of them.)

★ Take Pride in America
P.O. Box 1339-B
Jessup, MD 20794
(Write for information about how an organization can help save public lands. A class or youth organization might want to get involved.)

★ C.A.R.E.I.R.S.
P.O. Box 8900
Silver Spring, MD 20907
(The Conservation and Renewable Energy Inquiry Referral Service offers a free pamphlet entitled "Learning About Energy Conservation.")

★ The National Energy Foundation
5160 Wiley Post Way, Suite 200
Salt Lake City, UT 84116
(To find out about nuclear energy, write for a free copy of "The Nuclear Energy Energist," which includes a word search and a Nuclear Bingo Game.)

★ Greenpeace
1436 U Street N.W.
Washington, D.C. 20009

★ Greenpeace Foundation
240 Fort Mason
San Francisco, CA 94123
(Save the Whales and Dolphin project)

★ Whale Adoption Project
International Wildlife Coalition
320 Gifford Street
Falmouth, MA 02540
(This program helps support marine mammal research and teaches students about these animals. For $15, a class or family can "adopt" a whale.)

★ Save the Manatee Club
500 N. Maitland Avenue
Maitland, FL 32751
(A $10 membership fee goes toward research and the publication of a newsletter which provides information about manatees. The fee also allows you to adopt an individual manatee, and receive its photo and biography.)

Science Activities

➤ **A study of erosion:** Find two boxes of the same size (approximately 8" x 12" x 6" deep), and replace one end of each with screening to allow for drainage. Fill each box with soil, and shape mountains and hills on the sides and in the corners. Make a valley running down the middle of each box toward the screening. Make houses and trees if you want. Plant one box with grass seed and leave the other bare. Let the grass grow for 2 or 3 weeks, watering as directed on the bag of seed. Clip the grass, and water each box lightly with a watering can. Watch how the water runs off in each box. Which lost the most soil and water? What does this tell you about erosion and the importance of vegetation?

➤ **Acid rain:** Acid rain, snow and fog have killed fish and other aquatic life and noticeably damaged forests in areas of the United States, Canada, and Europe. Harmful chemicals which enter the air (industrial emissions, automobile exhaust, and so on) return to Earth in the form of acid rain, fog and snow, contaminating water and soil, and damaging buildings. It is a serious problem facing the planet.

Obtain some pHydrion (pH) papers from a school chemistry lab or a medical supply company. By dipping one of the small indicator strips into a solution, and comparing the color of the wet pH paper with the color chart that comes with the papers, you can determine whether the solution is acidic or alkaline. Test tap water, rain water, lemon juice, milk, ammonia, and so on. Record your results.

If you live in an area where acid rain is known to be a problem, you can test the effect of acid rain on plants. Start two plants from seeds, and care for them in exactly the same way except for watering. Water one with tap water and the other with rain water (use equal amounts). Keep a record of the progress of each plant.

Making It rain: For this, you will need a dish, a large jar, cold water, and hot water. Carefully put hot water in the jar and then pour most of it out. The air above the remaining water will be warm and humid. Now place a dish filled with cold water on top of the jar. Drops of water will form as the warm moist air is cooled by contact with the cold dish. As the drops become large, they fall like rain to the bottom of the jar.

Listen to weather reports for a description of the weather conditions which are expected to cause rain. Notice the similarities between the conditions which cause rain to fall from the sky and the conditions created in your kitchen "rain."

Insulation slows the rate at which ice melts. Not too many years ago, people cut ice from ponds and lakes during the winter and packed it in sawdust in ice-houses. Later, during the summer, they had ice when they needed it. Your child can experiment to see how long he can keep ice from melting. Encourage him to try different kinds of insulating materials to determine which one keeps the ice the longest.

> **Air pressure:** Fill a glass with water. Place a piece of heavy, smooth paper or cardboard over the top of the glass, completely covering the opening. Working over a sink or bucket, hold the card in place and invert the glass. The card should stay in place, the water remaining in the glass. This happens because of air pressure.

> **Grow a mold garden:** Using a metal or plastic container about 6 inches in diameter and 3 inches deep, firmly pack an inch-deep layer of moist garden soil into the bottom of your container. Choose food for your molds from the kitchen garbage — potato peelings, stale bread, an apple core, a banana peel. (Avoid cheese or meats, as they cause odors.) Place 5 pieces of food on the surface of your soil. Use small pieces, no bigger than half an inch square and only 1/8 to 1/4 inch thick. Cover the container with thin, transparent plastic and secure with a rubber band.

Remove the cover for a few minutes every few days to provide a good oxygen supply, and to check the soil. If it is too dry, you can moisten it. Your molds may be white, green, red, orange, or any color!

Try introducing different variables to determine the effects of heat and cold, and light and dark on mold growth. After a week or two, the molds may begin to disappear, and small nematode worms may be seen. These feed on the bacteria which grew on the molds and on the molds themselves. What you observe in your mold garden is what happens in a well-aerated compost pile.

> **Make a wormery:** Place worms in a gallon jar filled with alternate layers of soil, leaf mold and sand, and with grass seed planted on top. (Add a little water after each layer.) Cover the jar with black cloth or paper for a week to encourage the worms to tunnel near the sides. Twice a week feed them with small bits of leafy vegetables and some cornmeal or oats.

> **Bernouilli's Principle:** When I was 13 or 14, I asked my father, "Dad, how does a plane fly? How does it get off the ground if it's so heavy?" My father, a Naval test pilot for 12 years, drew several sketches to illustrate the basic concept behind flying. When I began teaching

sixth grade science, I discovered that the concept had a name: Bernouilli's Principle. Below is a simple experiment which will demonstrate the principle to your child.

Cut a drinking straw two thirds of the way through its width and bend it to make a right angle. Place the straw in a glass of juice as shown below, with one end below the surface of the juice.

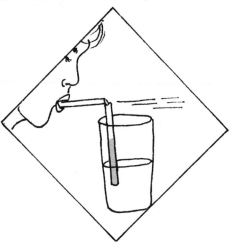

Blow into the horizontal half. The juice should rise as you blow the stream of air across the top of the straw. (You may have to experiment with positions of the straw to make it work.) Blowing makes the air above the straw's opening move faster and exert less pressure. The higher pressure of the air above the rest of the juice in the glass pushes it up the straw. It is a similar reduction of air pressure above the wing of an airplane that creates the "lift" enabling the craft to rise in the air.

How does yeast work? Mix 3 tablespoons of sugar in a half cup of warm water until the sugar disappears. Add 3 small packages of active dry yeast. Stir, and pour into a quart bottle. Stretch the opening of a balloon over the bottle mouth, and secure the balloon with a rubber band. Put the bottle in a warm place. The yeast cells eat the sugar for fuel and form a gas, carbon dioxide. When that gas is released, it inflates the balloon. Now when you bake bread, your child will have a better understanding of how the dough rises!

You might like to try a few other methods of blowing up a balloon. For these, use an empty soft drink bottle (16 oz.).

★ Hold a bottle with a balloon fastened on top, under hot water.

★ Put some baking soda in a bottle and vinegar in a balloon. Carefully fasten the balloon over the top of the bottle and then dump the vinegar in.

★ Try the same experiment as above but with several Alka Seltzer tablets in the bottle and water in the balloon.

Were you able to blow up the balloon in each case? Which method worked the best?

Air

▶ Turn an empty glass upside down in a bowl 2/3 full of water. Does the glass fill with water? Why not?

▶ Set birthday candles (already lit) in lumps of clay under jars of different sizes. Time how long each candle continues burning. Graph the results, putting number of ounces (size of jars) along one side, and amount of time the candle burned along the other.

▶ Attach the mouth of a deflated balloon to the mouth of a clean, dry soda bottle, with the balloon on the inside of the bottle. Try to blow up the balloon. (No matter how hard you try, you can't blow up the balloon, because air is resisting the balloon so that it cannot expand.)

▶ **Grow rock candy crystals:** Tie a button to a string and attach the string to a pencil or stick. Set the pencil across the top of a glass, with the button suspended in the glass. Mix 2 1/2 cups of sugar in 1 cup of water and heat until the syrup boils. Cook over medium heat, without stirring, for 3 to 4 minutes. (Caution: the syrup is extremely hot!)

Remove and let the syrup cool a minute or two before pouring into the glass. (If it's too hot, it will break the glass.)

Let the glass sit somewhere, undisturbed but easy to see, for a week or more. Crystals will begin to form around the string. These tiny, perfect "starter crystals" will turn into larger, more irregular chunks. When they are large enough, break off a piece and eat!

> **Twenty questions:** Start by thinking of any object that strikes your fancy, say a potato. Teach your child to ask only questions which can be answered with a "yes" or a "no." The first several questions should be used to narrow the object down to one of three main categories. "Is it an animal?" No. "Is it a mineral?" No. "Is it a vegetable?" Yes. And so on from there. This game is valuable in that it teaches a child to consider attributes, alternatives and categories, and to narrow down the field of possibilities until he discovers the identity of the object.

> **Outdoor scavenger hunt:** This is most fun if you have a group of children and can form teams. Give each team a paper sack, a list like the one below, and a time limit for finding the different items listed.

★ a dead leaf

★ something red

★ a smooth stone

★ a feather

★ a seed

★ a small twig

★ something alive

★ a piece of bark

★ a piece of litter

★ a flowering weed

> There are a number of publications which offer fun science activities which can be done using everyday materials found in the home. They provide opportuni-

ties for parents and children to spend time together, having fun with science and with each other.

▶ *WONDERSCIENCE* is a quarterly 8-page publication filled with activities and experiments for children in grades 4-6. For a one-year subscription, send $4.00 to: *WONDERSCIENCE*, American Chemical Society, P.O. Box 57136, West End Station, Washington, D.C. 20037.

▶ Look in the library or send for *The Original Backyard Scientist* and *Backyard Scientist, Series One*, by Jane Hoffman. Each book is filled with activities for children ages 4-12. For information on ordering, write: Backyard Scientist, P.O. Box 16966, Irvine, CA 92713.

▶ The Smithsonian Institute offers a large (16"x32") "Family Learning Project Science Calendar" which suggests activities based on materials generally found in the home. The activities have also been compiled in book form. For information about the calendar or books, contact: Galison Books, Dept. #3, 25 West 43rd St., New York, NY 10036; Phone: (212) 354-8840.

▶ *The Kids' Nature Book* by Susan Milord offers activities to help parents involve their children in science in some way every day of the year. Activities follow week-long themes, and teach children about topics from meteors to insects to plants to weather. For information about ordering, write Williamson Publishing Co., P.O. Box 185, Church Hill Road, Charlotte, VT 05445, or call 1-800-234-8791.

Geography

EIGHT

Geography

One day I asked my class to try and name all fifty of the United States. When I heard "Japan" offered with a straight face, I knew the child was serious. When there were no chuckles or expressions of surprise from the other students, I knew that the child was not alone in his ignorance of geography.

I was disturbed to find that so many sixth graders could be that unaware of the world and their place in it. Since that day, however, I have read on a number of occasions about studies which reveal that the problem is neither new nor is it confined to our country. In a newspaper article dated August 4, 1988, Jack Kilpatrick describes the findings of a survey conducted in the spring of that year among 10,820 people in nine countries. The survey was commissioned by the National Geographic Society and the questions were asked of adults, almost 80 percent of whom had at least a high school education. Consider the following about the U.S. respondents:

★ 25 percent did not know north from south, or east from west.

★ Barely half could locate the state of New York.

★ On a world map, the United States was "located" in China, India, the Soviet Union, Australia, Brazil and Botswana.

★ 23 percent could not locate the Pacific Ocean.

★ Looking at a map of South America, more than half could identify only one country, Brazil.

The survey also found that few considered geography to be dull. Most found geography either somewhat interesting or very interesting, and wished they'd had more of it.

Advances in technology and efforts to solve the world's environmental problems are drawing people from many countries closer together. The likelihood of working with people from other countries increases all the time. Therefore, it is important that our children have a good understanding of the world and their place in it. Not only should they be aware of the location of as many different countries as possible, but they should also have an understanding of the various resources, economies, climates, cultures, religions, and races around the globe.

Parents can easily increase a child's geography skills and make the study of different countries and peoples interesting. Here are some ideas and activities to get you started.

Geography Activities

One thing I distinctly remember about my best friend's house was that two walls of the family room were taken up by maps — one of the world, the other of the United States. I remember locating places that we had visited or where relatives lived or places we had heard about in the news. The ready availability of the maps helped us develop a comfortable familiarity with geography.

I heartily recommend that you invest in both U.S. and world maps for your home. (Wall maps are quicker and easier to use than an atlas, although I hope you will also add an atlas to your home library if you don't already have one.) Office supply stores usually carry nice, big folded maps that can be tacked to a wall for easy reference. Be sure you mount them low enough for your child to see easily.

➤ Talk about your child's "world" as it relates to the larger world. Ask your child to tell you his address. Then ask him the following questions:

★ What street do we live on?

★ What city/town do we live in?

★ What county is our city in?

★ What state do we live in?

★ What country do we live in?

★ What countries border the United States?

★ What continent do we live on?

★ What hemisphere do we live in?

★ What planet do we live on?

➤ Have your child draw a map of your neighborhood or how to get from your house to school. Then, get in the car and follow his map.

➤ Discuss the idea of our country being made up of fifty states. Does your child know how many are in the continental U.S.? What two other states are also included in our country?

➤ For fun one day, sit down and see if you and your child, or even better, your whole family, can name all 50 states. This is a great car game. For more advanced geographers, try adding state capitals!

➤ Consider buying a jigsaw-type puzzle of the United States. Puzzles are a fun way to become familiar with the names, shapes and locations of the states. Be sure your child realizes that at this point you are just focusing on one country, our own, and that there are many other countries in the world.

➤ As you concentrate on the U.S., point out important physical features such as the Great Lakes, Mississippi River, Gulf of Mexico, Rocky Mountains, Appalachian Mountains, Great Plains, and so on. You can eventually describe and study individual states and groups of states such as New England, the South, etc. Discuss how climate, resources, agriculture and economy are affected by the location and physical features of an area.

➤ Help your child learn to identify and locate the seven continents in the world. He should also be able to locate the Atlantic, Pacific and Indian Oceans.

➤ Explain the theory of "continental drift" which hypothesizes that at one time in the earth's history, all land was one large mass that has since broken apart into pieces or continents. Point out how, if you pushed South America east until it touched Africa, you could almost fit them together like the pieces of a puzzle. Try to discover other places which could have fit together long ago. Draw the continents and try putting them together like puzzle pieces.

➤ Be sure your child understands the concepts of north, south, east and west, and can figure out what direction is indicated by NE, NW, SE and SW as well. Make a game of it by identifying landmarks in your town (Is your school north or east of your house?) and by watching highway signs (Do we want to take the highway east or west to get to Grandma's?).

➤ Get out some road maps and let your child choose a route to get from one place to another. This is a great activity if you are planning a real trip. Otherwise, pretend you are going to take a vacation. Let your child choose a destination. Discuss the way the map is scaled, how for instance one inch on the map might represent 500 miles of territory. Throw in a math lesson by asking what distance one and a half inches would represent. Help to measure the total distance and figure the mileage. Figure out about how long the trip will take, considering the mileage and a traveling speed of 55 miles an hour. You might add time for rest stops and eating, to make it more realistic.

➤ Discuss the purpose of the "key" (or legend) on a map. Explain the symbols found on the various maps you have. Usually the capital of a state or country is represented by a star. Sometimes the capital's name is underlined instead. Road maps may have symbols for state parks, bridges, railroads, and historical monuments as well as roads and highways.

➤ Encourage your child to watch the news with you in the evening. Make it a game to see how many names of cities, counties, states, and countries you hear. Locate the different places on a map.

➤ If your child develops an interest in a particular country, encourage him to write to travel agencies, embassies, and offices of tourism and ask for free information, posters, and so on.

➤ Look on toys, canned foods and other products to see where they were manufactured or processed. What might influence where something is produced? Consider starting an informal list by country on the bulletin board. Write down each item that originates in a particular country. What kinds of economies do you see?

➤ Your child might want to start a collection of objects from different countries around the world. A few ideas are stamps, coins, and dolls. If you have relatives or neighbors who travel to other countries from time to time, encourage your child to ask them to bring back samples of foreign currency — paper and coin. Or he might offer to give them some money with which to purchase a variety of stamps.

➤ Play "Where Am I?" by giving hints which describe a geographical location. The person who guesses the location gets to give the clues next. For example, "I am very hot. The area around here is parched. Someone said it is the lowest place below sea level. Where am I?" (the Dead Sea).

➤ Help your child make a map of his bedroom. This may sound simple to you, but for someone who has never had to imagine "looking down" into a room, it is not that easy. Help with the placement of the objects and understanding spatial organization.

➤ Whenever your child needs a map for a report or project, encourage him to draw his own. Drawing a map freehand is a far more valuable learning experience than cutting out a map from a magazine or even tracing.

Creative Geography

★ A good weekend project is to make a topographical map of the United States (or one particular state or a foreign country) using plaster of Paris on a piece of plywood or heavy-duty cardboard. Have your child draw the outline first and keep a map beside him to refer to as he creates mountains, plateaus, rivers, etc. Remind him to mix small amounts of plaster and work on only one area at a time, as the plaster dries quickly. Once the map is dry, it can be painted.

★ Help your child make a pizza in the shape of the United States or of a particular state or country. Add sauce and toppings to mark features such as rivers, lakes, mountains, as well as cities where friends or relatives live or favorite vacation spots.

Things You Can Send For

★ A variety of maps are available at low cost from the United States Geological Survey. For a free catalog, write to: U.S.G.S. Map Sales, Box 25286, Denver, CO 80225, and ask for their free "Catalog of Maps."

★ Hammond publishes a series of comic books entitled "Captain Atlas and the Globe Riders." They are scientifically accurate atlases in comic book form, written for children ages 8 and up, and cost $6.95 each. Call toll free: 800-526-4953.

★ To obtain a map showing whale populations, send a check for $2.50 (made payable to Treasurer of the United States), to Defense Mapping Agency, CSC, Attn.: PMSR, Washington, D.C. 20315-0020, or call 800-826-0342.

★ For a map showing where dinosaurs roamed, send a check for $3.95 to The American Museum of Natural History, The Museum Shop, Central Park West at 79th Street, New York, NY 10024, or call (212) 769-5150.

Appendix

Sources of Information on Middle Schools:

ASCD Working Group on the Emergent Adolescent Learner. *The Middle School We Need.* Arlington, VA: ASCD, 1975

Atwell, Nancie. *In The Middle: Writing, Reading and Learning with Adolescents.* Upper Montclair, NJ: Boynton/Cook, 1987

Eichorn, Donald. *The Middle School.* New York: Center for Applied Research, 1968

Elkind, David. *All Grown Up and No Place to Go: Teenagers in Crisis.* Reading, MA: Addison-Wesley, 1984

Lipsitz, Joan. *Successful Schools for Young Adolescents.* New Brunswick, NJ: Transaction Books, 1984

Thornburg, Hershel D., Editor. *Preadolescent Development.* Tuscon, Arizona: The University of Arizona Press, 1974

School Readiness

Ready or Not! The School Readiness Handbook (revised 1988) offers a checklist which can help parents determine if their child is ready for first grade. Also included is a kindergarten readiness checklist. To obtain the handbook, send $7 to Research Concepts, 1368 E. Airport Road, Muskegon, MI 49444. (Ask for the parents' kit.)

Cuisenaire Rods

Cuisenaire rods are one kind of manipulative that can be used to help introduce a child to basic math concepts. The "Math Made Meaningful" kit includes 155 rods, 50 topic cards and a teacher's manual with activity ideas for working with preschool through elementary school age children. As of the date of this book's publication, the price for the kit is $26.95 for a set of wooden rods, and $24.95 for a set of plastic rods. Add 8% of the total to cover postage and handling.

Cuisenaire Co. of America
12 Church Street, Box D
New Rochelle, New York 10802
Phone: (914) 235-0900

Children's Magazines

Subscribing to a magazine for your child is a great way to tie reading to a pleasant occasion - that of receiving mail. Magazines offer stories, puzzles, and activity ideas as well as interesting and useful information. Keep in mind that different magazines appeal to different children. Each is written for a specific age group and more often than not, focuses on a particular subject area. Below is a list of magazines to consider. You may want to write for a sample issue of several different magazines and let your child choose which he'd most like to subscribe to.

Chickadee (for ages 3 to 8) and *Owl* (for ages 9 to 12) are both published by Canada's Young Naturalist Foundation, and include articles involving a variety of areas of science. Each also offers activity ideas along with humor and art. For subscription information, write to *Chickadee* or *Owl*, 255 Great Arrow

Avenue, Box 4, Buffalo, NY 14207. For a sample, send $2.50 to the address given.

Cricket is a literary magazine for children ages 6 to 12. Each issue includes stories and artwork from well-known and respected authors and illustrators. *Cricket* also includes games, jokes, and letters. For subscription information, write *Cricket*, P.O. Box 51144, Boulder, CO 80321, or call 800-435-6850. For a sample, send $2.50 to the address given.

Games Junior for ages 6 to 12, this includes lots of puzzles, games of logic, and activities which encourage creative thinking. For subscription information, write *Games Junior*, 810 Seventh Avenue, New York, NY 10102, or call 800-777-1888.

Kid City, from the publishers of *Sesame Street Magazine*, is for 6 to 10-year-olds and offers a variety of activities, stories, puzzles, and interesting articles. For subscription information, write Kid City, P.O. Box 51277, Boulder, CO 80321 or call 800- 525-0643. For a sample, send $1.50 to *Sesame Street Magazine*, Children's Television Workshop, One Lincoln Plaza, New York, NY 10023.

National Geographic World, for children age 8 to 13, like its parent, *National Geographic*, includes wonderful photography along with articles which focus on science, natural history, geography and anthropology. For subscription information, write *National Geographic World*, P.O. Box 2330, Washington, DC 20077, or call 800-638-6400. For a free sample, write to 17th and M Streets, Washington, DC 20036.

Odyssey, for children 8 to 14 years old, focuses on astronomy and space exploration, offering informative articles as well as helpful advice for amateur astronomers. For subscription information, write Odyssey, 1027 North Seventh Street, Milwaukee, WI 53233. For a sample issue, send a self-addressed 8-1/2"x12" envelope with $1.25 postage to the address given.

Penny Power, written for 8 to 14 year-olds, is aimed at educating children as consumers. In addition to rating products which children are apt to buy, it also includes articles on a wide variety of topics. For subscription information, write Penny Power, Box 51777, Boulder, CO 80321, or call 800-234-2078. For a sample, send $2 to the address given.

Ranger Rick, published by the National Wildlife Federation for 6 to 12 year-olds, includes great photographs along with articles which focus on ecology and conservation. For subscription information, write National Wildlife Federation, 1400 16th Street, N.W., Washington, DC 20036, or call 800-432-6564. For a sample issue, send $2 to the address given.

Sports Illustrated for Kids, like the well-known adult version, is a magazine for 8 to 12 year-olds which presents articles on young athletes, as well as Olympic and professional athletes, complete with large, color photos. For subscription information, write *Sports Illustrated for Kids*, P.O. Box 830609, Birmingham, AL 35282, or call 800-632-1300. A sample may be obtained by sending $1.75 to the address given.

*U*S*Kids*, from the publishers of *Weekly Reader*, for children age 5 to 10, includes lots of articles on real-life people, places and events, as well as puzzles to tease the brain. For subscription information, write *U*S*Kids*, P.O. Box 8957, Boulder, CO 80322, or call (800) 525-0643. For a sample issue, send $2.25 to the address given.

3-2-1 Contact is aimed at children ages 8 to 14, who are especially interested in math and science. For subscription information, write *3-2-1 Contact*, E=MC Square, P.O. Box 51177, Boulder, CO 80321, or call 800-525-0643. For a sample issue, send $1.50 to One Lincoln Plaza, New York, NY 10023.

Bibliography

Ames, Louise Bates; and Ilg, Frances L.; and Baker, Sidney M. *Your Ten-to-Fourteen-Year-Old*. New York: Delacorte Press, 1988.

Ames, Louise Bates. *Questions Parents Ask: Straight Answers From Louise Bates Ames, Ph.D.* New York: Clarkson N. Potter, Inc., Publishers, 1988.

Armstrong, Thomas. *In Their Own Way: Discovering and Encouraging Your Child's Personal Learning Style*. Los Angeles: Jeremy P. Tarcher, Inc., 1987.

___. "Other Forms of Intelligence." *Parenting*, November 1988.

___. "The Art of the Matter." *Parenting*, June/July 1989.

Ballinger, Susan. "Make a Moon Calendar." *Science Scope*, February/March 1988.

Beck, Melinda. "Can't Spell? Yur Not Dumm." *Newsweek*, June 6, 1988.

Bernstein, Joanne E. and Mona Behan. "Good Reads." *Parenting*, June/July 1989.

Bjorklund, David and Barbara Bjorklund. "Is Your Child Ready For School?" *Parents*, June 1988.

Brady, James. "In Step With: Jimmy Stewart." *Parade Magazine*, August 20, 1989.

Brandt, Anthony. "Read All About It." *Parenting*, October 1988.

___. "Sex and the Facts of Math." *Parenting*, December 1988/January 1989.

Briggs, Dorothy Corkille. *Your Child's Self-Esteem*. Garden City, New York: Doubleday & Company, Inc., 1970.

Canfield, Jack and Harold C. Wells. *100 Ways to Enhance Self-Concept in the Classroom*. Englewood Cliffs, New Jersey: Prentice-Hall, Inc., 1976.

Carlinsky, Dan. *Do You Know Your Parents?* Los Angeles: Price, Stern, Sloan, 1982.

Chall, Jeanne S. *Stages of Reading Development*. New York: McGraw-Hill Book Co., 1983.

Challand, Helen J. *Activities in the Life Sciences*. Chicago: Childrens Press, 1982.

___. *Science Projects and Activities*. Chicago: Childrens Press, 1985.

Cohen, Dorothy H. *The Learning Child: Guidelines for Parents & Teachers*. New York: Vintage Books, 1972.

Comer, James P. "Money Management." *Parents*, June 1985.

Costello, Joan. "Money Talk." *Parents*, November 1984.

Dodson, Fitzhugh. *How To Discipline With Love (From Crib to College)*. New York: A Signet Book, 1978.

Donovan, Edward P. "Singular Peanuts." *Science Scope*, January 1989.

Dunn, Rita. "Suggestions for Starting With Style." Learning Styles Network Newsletter, Spring, 1986.

Dunn, Rita and Dunn, Kenneth. *Teaching Students Through Their Individual Learning Styles: A Practical Approach.* Reston, Virginia: Reston Publishing Co., Inc., 1978.

Dunn, Rita and Griggs, Shirley A. *Learning Styles: Quiet Revolution in American Secondary Schools.* Reston, Virginia: National Association of Secondary School Principals, 1988.

Eichen, Marc. "Bringing Maps Home." *Parents*, September 1989.

Elkind, David. *The Hurried Child: Growing Up Too Fast Too Soon.* Reading, Massachusetts: Addison-Wesley Publishing Co., 1981.

Environmental Defense Fund. "If You're Not Recycling You're Throwing It All Away." pamphlet published by EDF, 1988.

Freeman, Judy. *Books Kids Will Sit Still For: A Guide to Using Children's Literature for Librarians, Teachers and Parents.* Hagerstown, Maryland: The Alleyside Press, 1984.

Freeman, Mae and Ira. *Fun With Science.* New York: Random House, 1956.

Hayes, Marnell L. *The Tuned-In Turned-On Book About Learning Problems.* San Rafael, California: Academic Therapy, 1974.

Hirsch, Thomas L. *Puzzles for Pleasure and Leisure.* New York: Abelard-Schuman, 1966.

James, Elizabeth and Barkin, Carol. *How to Be School Smart: Secrets of Successful Schoolwork.* New York: Lothrop, Lee & Shepard Books, 1988.

Johnson, June. *838 Ways to Amuse a Child: Crafts, Hobbies and Creative Ideas for the Child From Six to Twelve.* New York: Harper Colophon Books, 1983.

Kaye, Peggy. *Games For Math: Playful Ways to Help Your Child Learn Math, From Kindergarten to Third Grade.* New York: Pantheon Books, 1987.

Kilpatrick, Jack. "We're too dumb about geography!" *Arkansas Democrat*, August 4, 1988.

Kolata, Gina. "Math is Only New When the Teacher Doesn't Get It." *The New York Times*, April 2, 1989.

Larrick, Nancy. *A Parent's Guide to Children's Reading.* Philadelphia: The Westminster Press, 1982.

Lemmon, Patricia. "A School Where Learning Styles Make A Difference." *The Principal*, Vol. 64, No. 4, March, 1985.

Maeroff, Gene I. "The Measure of a Good School." *Parenting*, May, 1989.

Marzollo, Jean. *SUPERKIDS: Creative Learning Activities for Children 5-15.* New York: Harper & Row Publishers, 1981.

May, Lola. "Variety is the Spice of Fractions." *Teaching K-8*, April 1989.

McCarthy, Bernice. *The 4Mat System: Teaching to Learning Styles With Right/Left Mode Techniques.* Oak Brook, Illinois: EXCEL, Inc., 1980.

McCoy, Elin. "Where Have All The Children Gone?" *Parents*, May 1986.

McNees, Pat. "Whole-Child Learning." Parents, July 1986.

___. "Learning How to Learn." *The Washington Post*, February 12, 1985.

Miller, Christina G. and Berry, Louise A. *Acid Rain: A Sourcebook for Young People.* New York: Julian Messner, 1986.

Miller, Mary Susan. *Bringing Learning Home: How Parents Can Play a More Active and Effective Role in Their Children's Education.* New York: Harper & Row, Publishers, 1981.

Nelson, Don. "The Scientific Method: A Primer." *Science and Children*, May, 1988.

Nelson, Jane. *Positive Discipline: A Warm, Practical, Step-by-Step Sourcebook for Parents and Teachers*. New York: Ballantine Books, 1981, 1987.

Overholt, James L. *Dr. Jim's Elementary Math Prescriptions*. Santa Monica, California: Goodyear Publishing Co., Inc., 1978.

Palmer, Julia Reed and Schwabacher, Sara. *How to Start and Run a Book and Game Club: Make a Game of Reading and Math and Kids Will Play and Learn*. New York: American Reading Council, 1985.

Pomeranz, Virginia E., with Schultz, Dodi. "Vision Checkpoint," *Parents*, April 1985.

___. "Teachers Aren't Always Right." *Parents*, October 1984.

Problem Solving in Mathematics — Grades 5 and 6 (Lane County Mathematics Project). Eugene, Oregon: Lane Education Service District, 1983

Rich, Dorothy. *MegaSkills: How Families Can Help Children Succeed in School and Beyond*. Boston: Houghton Mifflin Company, 1988.

Riddle, Bob. "Night Time is the Right Time." *Science and Children*, November/December 1988.

Roberts, Francis. "Is Your Child Learning Disabled?" *Parents*, June 1985.

___. "The Lively Art of Science," *Parents*, October 1984.

___. "Should Parents Help With Homework?", *Parents*, October 1985.

___. "Why Spelling Is Hard", *Parents*, January 1985.

Roberts, Francis and Sheiffele, Wendy. "Does Your Child Need Speech Therapy?" *Parents*, October 1986.

Rosemond, John K. *Parent Power! A Common-Sense Approach to Raising Your Children in the Eighties*. New York: Pocket Books, 1981.

Rossman, Michael. "All in a Day's Walk." *Parenting*, May 1988.

Rubenstein, Mark, *The Growing Years: The New York Hospital-Cornell Medical Center Guide to Your Child's Emotional Development From Birth to Adolescence*. New York: Atheneum, 1987.

Rubin, Nancy. "Math Stinks!" *Parents*, June 1988.

Rutherford, Robert B., Jr. and Edgar, Eugene. *Teachers & Parents, A Guide to Interaction and Cooperation*. Boston: Allyn and Bacon, Inc., 1979.

Sagan, Carl. "Give Us Hope." *Parade Magazine*, November 27, 1988.

___. "Why We Need To Understand Science." *Parade Magazine*, September 10, 1989.

Samples, Bob; Hammond, Bill; and McCarthy, Bernice. *4Mat and Science: Toward Wholeness in Science Education*. Barrington, Illinois: EXCEL, Inc., 1985.

Sharp, Richard M.; Sharp, Vicki F.; and Solza, Anita C. *30 Math Games For the Elementary Grades*. Belmont, California: Fearon Publishers, 1974.

Shuttlesworth, Dorothy E. *The Story of Ants*. Garden City, New York: Doubleday & Company, Inc., 1964.

Smith, James A. *Creative Teaching of the Language Arts in the Elementary School*. Boston: Allyn and Bacon, 1967.

Smithsonian Family Learning Project. *Science Activity Book*. New York: Galison Books, 1987.

Sombke, Laurence. "Cut the Garbage." *U.S.A. Weekend*, April 21-23, 1989.

Stock, Gregory. *The Kids' Book of Questions*. New York: Workman Publishing, 1988.

Sunburst Communications. "The Gentle Art of Saying No." Pleasantville, New York, 1979.

Thornburg, Hershel D., ed. *Preadolescent Development*. Tuscon, Arizona: The University of Arizona Press, 1974.

Tilling, Thomas. "Teaching Kids to Save." *Parents*, July 1985.

Trelease, Jim. *The Read-Aloud Handbook*. New York: Penguin Handbooks, 1982.

Vail, Pricilla L. *Smart Kids With School Problems: Things to Know and Ways to Help*. New York: E.P. Dutton, 1987.

von Oech, Roger. *A Whack On the Side of the Head: How to Unlock Your Mind for Innovation*. New York: Warner Books, 1983.

Webster, David. Brain Boosters: *A Book of Exasperating Nature and Science Puzzles*. Garden City, NY: The Natural History Press, 1966.

Weissbourd, Bernice. "Signs of Vision and Hearing Problems." *Parents*, July 1985.

Welsh, Patrick. "What Parents Should Do For Their Kids." *U.S. News & World Report, Inc.*, May 26, 1986.

Wiener, Harvey. *Any Child Can Write: How to Improve Your Child's Writing Skills*. New York: McGraw-Hill Book Co., 1978.

More good books from
WILLIAMSON PUBLISHING

To order additional copies of *More Parents Are Teachers, Too*, please enclose $10.95 per copy plus $2.00 shipping and handling. Follow "To Order" instructions below. Thank you.

PARENTS ARE TEACHERS, TOO:
Enriching Your Child's First Six Years
by Claudia Jones

Be the best teacher your child ever has! Jones shares hundreds of ways to help any child learn in playful home situations. Lots on developing reading, writing, math skills. Plenty on creative and critical thinking, too. A book you'll love using!

192 pages, 6 x 9, illustrations, quality paperback, $9.95

THE KIDS' NATURE BOOK:
365 Indoor/Outdoor Activities and Experiences
by Susan Milord

Winner of the Parents' Choice Golden Award for learning and doing books, *The Kids' Nature Book* is loved by children, grandparents. and friends alike. Simple projects and activities emphasize fun while quietly reinforcing the wonder of the world.

160 pages, 12 x 9, 425 illustrations, quality paperback, $13.95

DOING CHILDREN'S MUSEUMS:
A Guide to 225 Hands-On Museums
by Joanne Cleaver

Turn and ordinary day into a spontaneous "vacation" by taking a child to some of the 225 participatory children's museums, discovery rooms, and nature centers covered in this highly acclaimed, one-of-a-kind book. Filled with museum specifics to help you pick and plan the perfect place for the perfect day.

224 pages, 6 x 9, quality paperback, $12.95

To Order:

At your bookstore or order directly from Williamson Publishing. We accept Visa and MasterCard (please include number and expiration date), or send check to:

Williamson Publishing Company
Church Hill Road, P.O. Box 185
Charlotte, Vermont 05445
Toll-free phone orders with credit cards:1-800-234-8791

Please add $2.00 for shipping. Satisfaction guaranteed!